To

e from

Ted & Mary
xx xx.

THE GARY VAUGHN GALLYHILL COLLECTION

Swanscombe
in old picture postcards

Christoph Bull BA (Hons). MCLIP, ALA.

eb
European Library *ZALTBOMMEL / THE NETHERLANDS*

ISBN 90 288 6746 5

Second edition, 2005: reprint of the original edition of 2004.

European Library
post office box 49
NL – 5300 AA Zaltbommel/The Netherlands
telephone: 0031 418 513144
fax: 0031 418 515515
e-mail:publisher@eurobib.nl

Introduction

Swanscombe is an ancient parish consisting of 2,142 acres (or 3.34 square miles) and it encompasses Swanscombe, Greenhithe and the former hamlets of Galley Hill, Milton Street, Knockhall and Western Cross. The north-east consists of flat marshes and the River Ebbsfleet marks much of the western boundary with its larger neighbour Northfleet. In the south is the ancient Watling Street, which marks the southern boundary with Southfleet, and Swanscombe's western neighbour is Stone. This book will largely ignore Greenhithe and concentrate on Swanscombe and her hamlets alone.

Swanscombe's great claim to fame is the Swanscombe Skull, three fragments of a female some 400,000 years old found in 1935, 1936 and 1955. Other important people of Swanscombe, whom we shall meet in this book, include Marie Stopes, Sir Erasmus Wilson and Sir Anthony Weldon.

Swanscombe experienced a huge change in the early years of Queen Victoria's reign when in one generation it changed from an agricultural community into a cement town. The population increased by 908.3 % between 1801 and 1911 (thanks to Geoff Baker for this statistic). The cement industry owned virtually the whole parish after 1872 and created vast pits, terraced housing and pollution as well as employment – the town's reaction to this was often in very radical politics and a determination to resist the sometimes unreasonable demands of the cement industry's appetite for profits.

Swanscombe is now in another time of change – the industry has gone but the Swanscombe it created is still a powerful social and architectural force. The government plans to redevelop the area of north-west Kent known as 'Kent Thameside' and this will be as great a change to the existing social and physical landscape of Swanscombe as the coming of the cement industry was after 1825.

This book attempts to capture a lost world, but one that is very much within living memory (the Cement Works only closed in 1990).
The book also hopes to help retain the close Swanscombe identity by reminding present and future generations of the lives and landscapes of their predecessors, and help them to measure and interpret the town, which they see before them now.

Acknowledgements

The late Alf Hall, Len Stoneham, my late aunt Margaret Bull, Mrs. Hazel, Mr. Jenns of Church Road, Councillor Malcolm Munn of Swanscombe & Greenhithe Town Council and John Oxford – all these people gave of their time and knowledge.
Dartford Library's 'Dartford & Hundred of Axstane Local Collection' was used extensively for sources of information and illustrations.

Dedications

To my wife Heather and my daughters Catherine and Sarah who often thought I was in Swanscombe even while being at home in Chalk, as I typed and wrote notes on the town. To my friends in Swanscombe, to the memory of old Swanscombe Branch Library in Church Road (1928-2002) and to my beloved late mother, Ilse Hildegard Ida Bull (nee Schultz, 1920-2002).

About the author

Christoph Bull was born and has lived in north-west Kent all his life. He has been interested in local history since a boy and has been interested in Swanscombe for some twenty years. While working as Local Studies Librarian at Dartford Library, he organised a very well attended series of events celebrating Swanscombe Library's 70th anniversary in 1998.
Christoph has worked as Local Studies Librarian at Gravesend 1982-1988, as Reference Librarian and later as Local Studies Librarian at Dartford 1988-1998. Since 1998 he has served on the library management team for west Kent. Christoph Bull has twice been president of Gravesend Historical Society and is currently vice-chairman of Dartford Historical & Antiquarian Society and president of Chalk Parish History Group. Christoph Bull was also vice-chairman of governors at Northcourt County Primary School in Denton – where he was once a pupil - (until its closure in 2003). Christoph and his family live in Chalk near Gravesend. Since October 2004 Christoph has been the DistrictManager of the Gravesham District of Kent Libraries and Archives.

Second edition September 2005

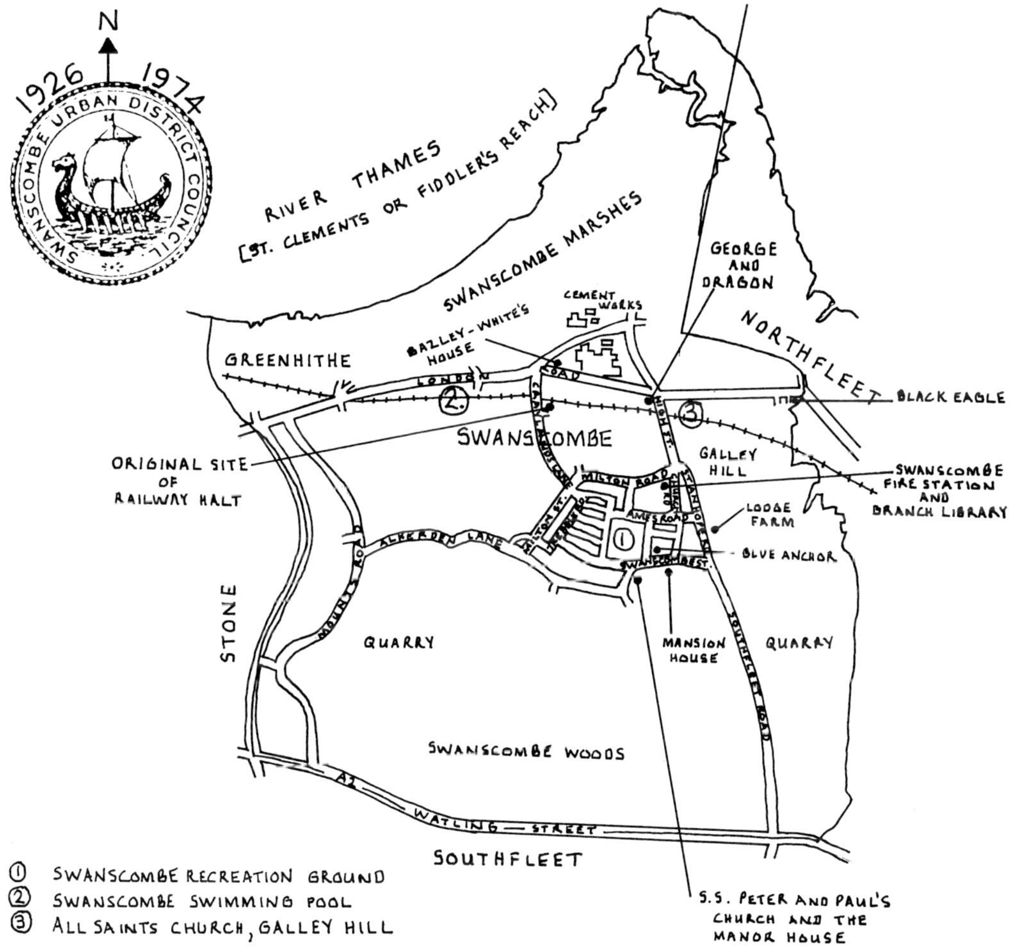
N
1926 1974
SWANSCOMBE URBAN DISTRICT COUNCIL
RIVER THAMES
[ST. CLEMENTS OR FIDDLER'S REACH]
SWANSCOMBE MARSHES
CEMENT WORKS
BAZLEY - WHITE'S HOUSE
GEORGE AND DRAGON
NORTHFLEET
BLACK EAGLE
GREENHITHE
LONDON ROAD
SWANSCOMBE
HIGH ST.
GALLEY HILL
ORIGINAL SITE OF RAILWAY HALT
MILTON ROAD
AMES ROAD
SWANSCOMBE FIRE STATION AND BRANCH LIBRARY
LODGE FARM
ALKERDEN LANE
SWANSCOMBE ST.
BLUE ANCHOR
STONE
QUARRY
MANSION HOUSE
QUARRY
SOUTHFLEET ROAD
SWANSCOMBE WOODS
A2
WATLING — STREET
SOUTHFLEET
S.S. PETER AND PAUL'S CHURCH AND THE MANOR HOUSE
① SWANSCOMBE RECREATION GROUND
② SWANSCOMBE SWIMMING POOL
③ ALL SAINTS CHURCH, GALLEY HILL

SWANSCOMBE–NORTHFLEET.

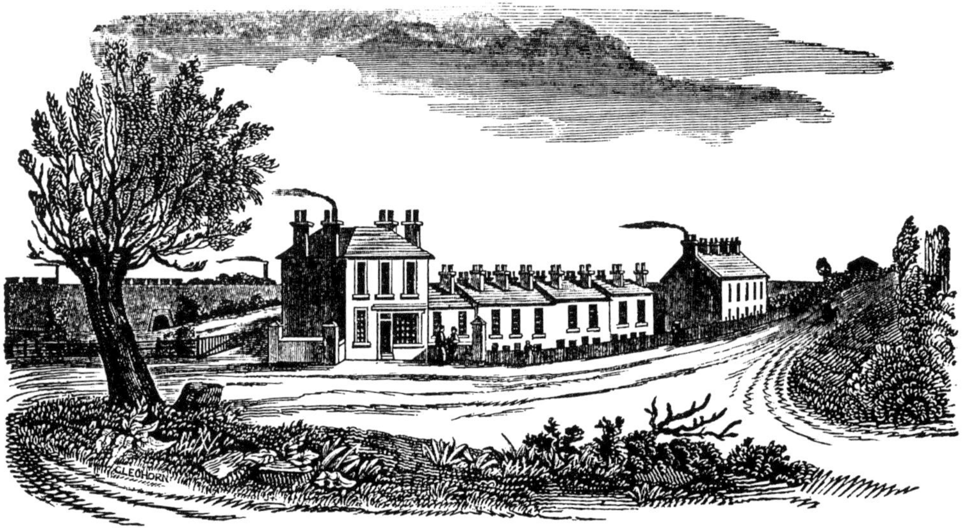

Estuary of the river Ebbs—wherein have lain the Roman & Danish Fleets.

1. Engraving: 'Swanscombe – Northfleet' 1854. This engraving was published by A.J. Dunkin (printer and historian of Dartford) in 1854. The buildings shown were then recently built – the left-hand building was the Black Eagle public house, which saw the huge changes to this area until its own closure in 1967. The changes included wartime bombing of Taunton Road, massive industrialisation and redevelopment. The hill in the picture is Galley Hill and the North Kent railway line (the tunnel shown still exists) is in the background, having opened in 1849. On the right of the picture is Lower Road, now leading to the Inveresk Industrial Estate (also known as the Northfleet Industrial Estate). In 1854 this latter road would have led to the Cement Works and was always a connection to Swanscombe Marshes. The view marks the boundary between Swanscombe and Northfleet: the tree in the front is in Northfleet – all else in Swanscombe.

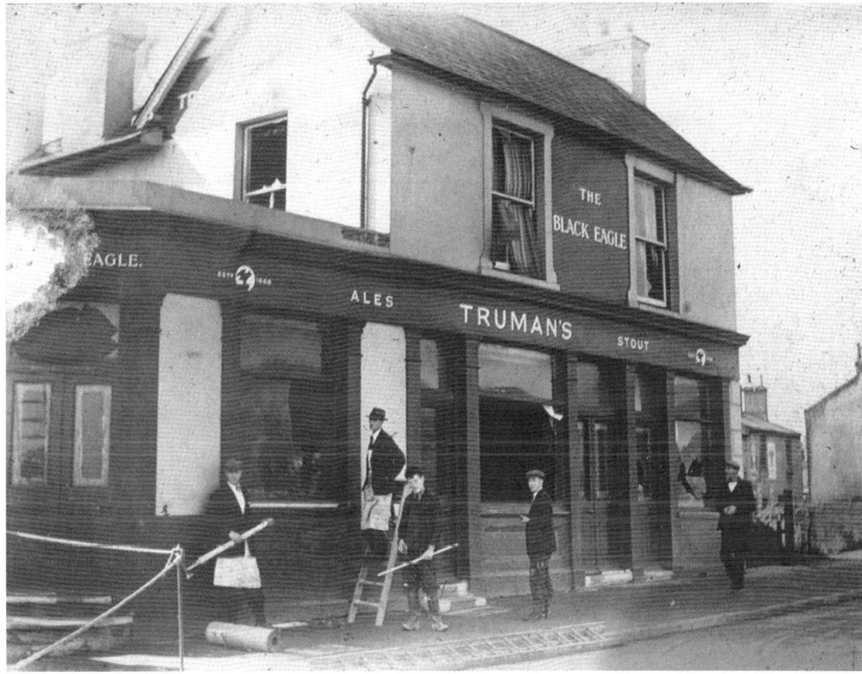

2. Black Eagle public house, Galley Hill circa 1944. Coming west from Northfleet along the A226, the Black Eagle was the first building inside Swanscombe Parish. The pub dates from about 1866 and served the Taunton Road community and the expanding industrial areas springing up on the Swanscombe/Northfleet border. As road traffic increased during the twentieth century, this corner became dangerous and saw many accidents. The Black Eagle was damaged on 30th July 1944 when a V1 (flying bomb) destroyed much property in Taunton Road and on the main road (killing 13 people and injuring 91). In the 1950s the pub had its saloon bar (left-hand side), jug and bottle (middle doors) and the public bar through the double doors at the front. The beer was held in high esteem because the best temperature was maintained by it being stored in the cellar cut out of chalk with no brick lining inside. The Black Eagle was demolished in 1968.

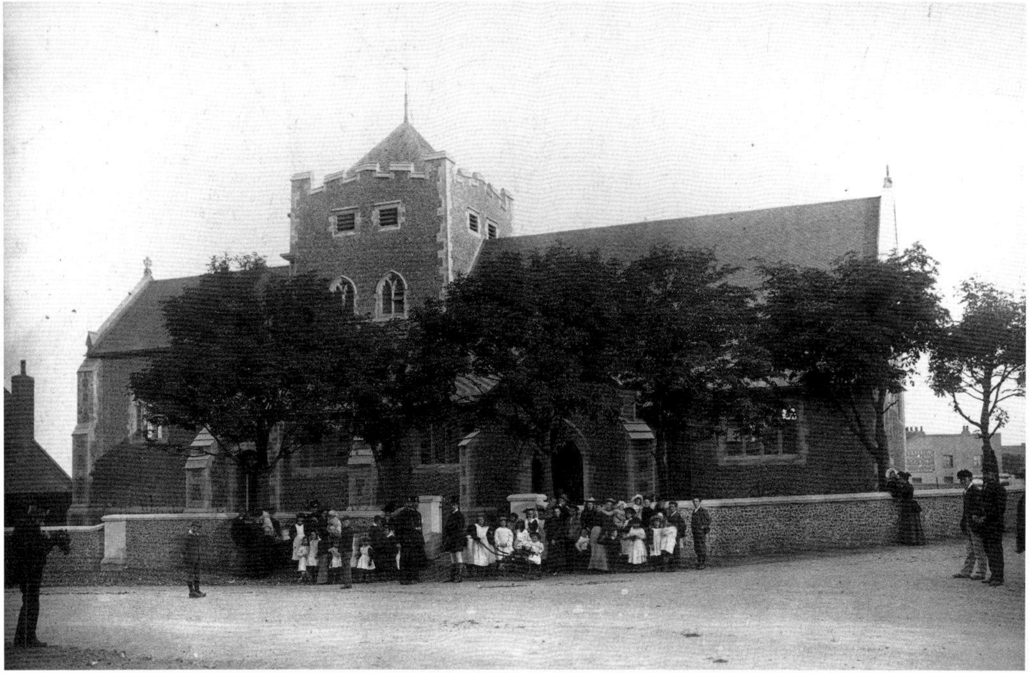

3. All Saint's Church, Galley Hill, 1894. This photograph appears to show Galley Hill Church shortly after the current building was constructed in 1894: the church's fabric appears to be very crisp and new. All Saint's was originally a corrugated iron construction on the opposite side of London Road and was created as a separate church parish from the original parish church of Swanscombe (Saint's Peter and Paul) in 1883. The huge growth of the Galley Hill area over the previous 30-40 years meant that what was a country lane to Swanscombe Street was now a busy bustling community which became the High Street we know today. Two county constabulary policemen are standing left of the entrance gate, with the Alma public house in the High Street (belonging to the Dartford Brewery Company) and the roofs of the houses in Orchard Street in the background. Orchard Street was completely redeveloped in the early 1950s and was one of the first slum clearance schemes in Swanscombe.

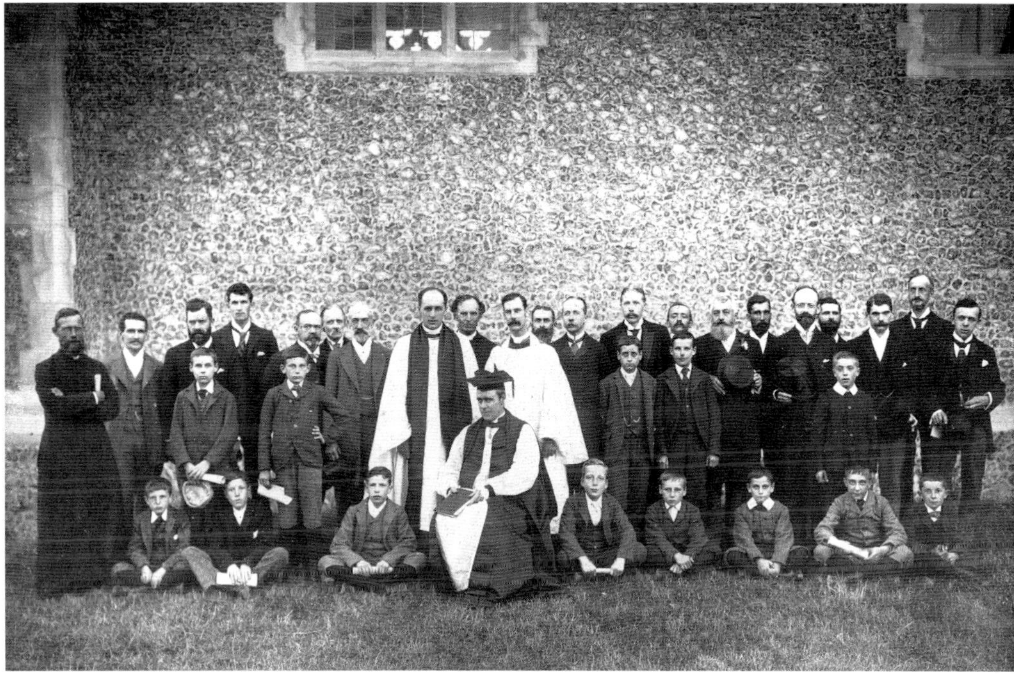

4. Clergy and guests at All Saint's Church, Galley Hill. This photograph was taken on 23 July 1895 when All Saint's Church had been completed and was being dedicated. The original corrugated iron building standing opposite was now used as a church house meeting room and for parish council meetings. The Bishop of Rochester, the Right Reverend Randall Thomas Davidson – bishop from 1891 till 1895, later Archbishop of Canterbury 1903-1928 – is seated with his mortarboard; mitres were seen as too papist for the Church of England at this time. To the bishop's right is Rev. Arthur F.C. Owen, vicar 1890-1900; and to his left is Canon Murray, Rural Dean and Rector of Stone. The other guests are local worthies including members of the White Family, Cement Works owners and major church benefactors. The gentleman who is fifth from the left standing is John Bazley White (1848-1927), along with Leedham White (1838-1905) 7th from left, and Frederick Anthony White (1842-1933) 12th from left. These men had enormous influence in Swanscombe because of their wealth and status as major employers and they saw the church as providing spiritual and moral guidance to their army of workers.

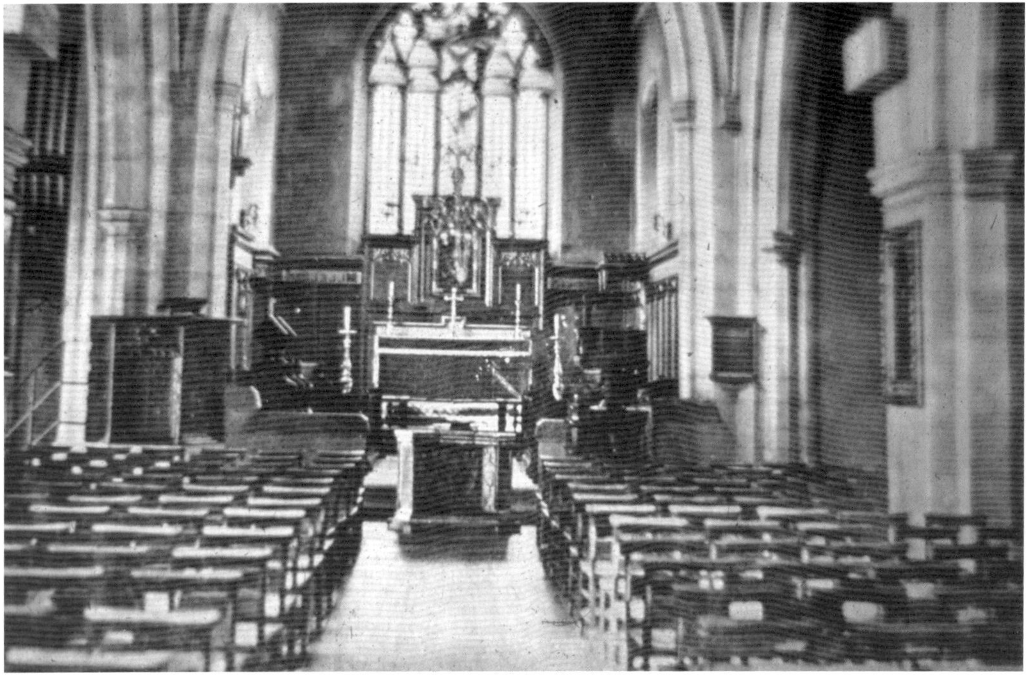

5. Interior of All Saint's, Galley Hill, circa 1935. This view shows the well-provided for church, which had so much help in its foundation from the White Family – owner of Swanscombe Cement Works. The architect was Richard Norman Shaw (1831-1912); a stained glass window was by Christopher Whall (1849-1921), a leader in the revival of post-medieval stained glass. The church was largely built with the financial aid given by Messrs. Leedham, John Bazley and Frederick Anthony White (see picture 4). It contained several art treasures including two paintings: a crucifixion by Jacopo da Carucci (1494-1556/7) and a Madonna with two children by Mariotto Albertinelli (1474-1515), a litany desk made from a sixteenth-century Spanish tabernacle and an eighteenth-century candelabrum. The treasures were removed to Saint Peter and Paul's Church when All Saint's was declared redundant by the Church of England in 1971, but some have been subsequently sold. In 1990 the empty building was tastefully converted into flats.

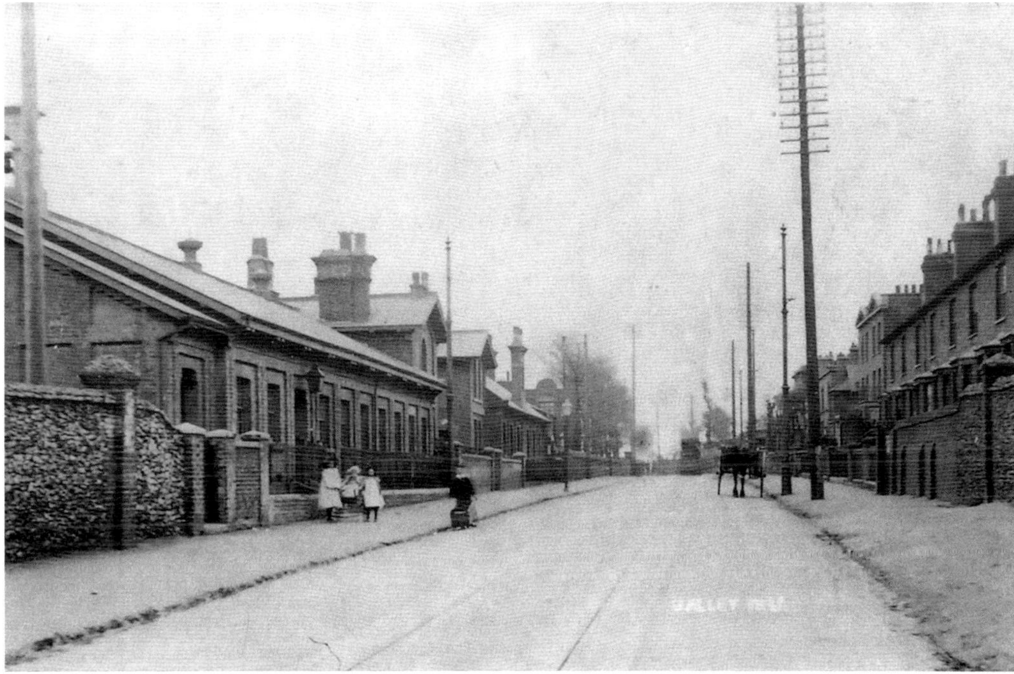

6. Galley Hill looking east, circa 1910. A view towards Northfleet with the George & Dragon public house on the furthest distance on the right. The terraced houses on the right dated from the 1850s and the vicarage for All Saint's Church was in the middle of this row. The North Kent railway line behind severely restricted the space for housing. On the left is Galley Hill School, built in 1858, which by 1913 could hold over six hundred children and which served the needs of the expanding cement factory population. Beyond on the left was the original 1882 iron All Saint's Church, later used as a church house and social club (called the 17th club, so named after Swanscombe's Home Guard Battalion). Virtually every building in this picture had been demolished by 1986.

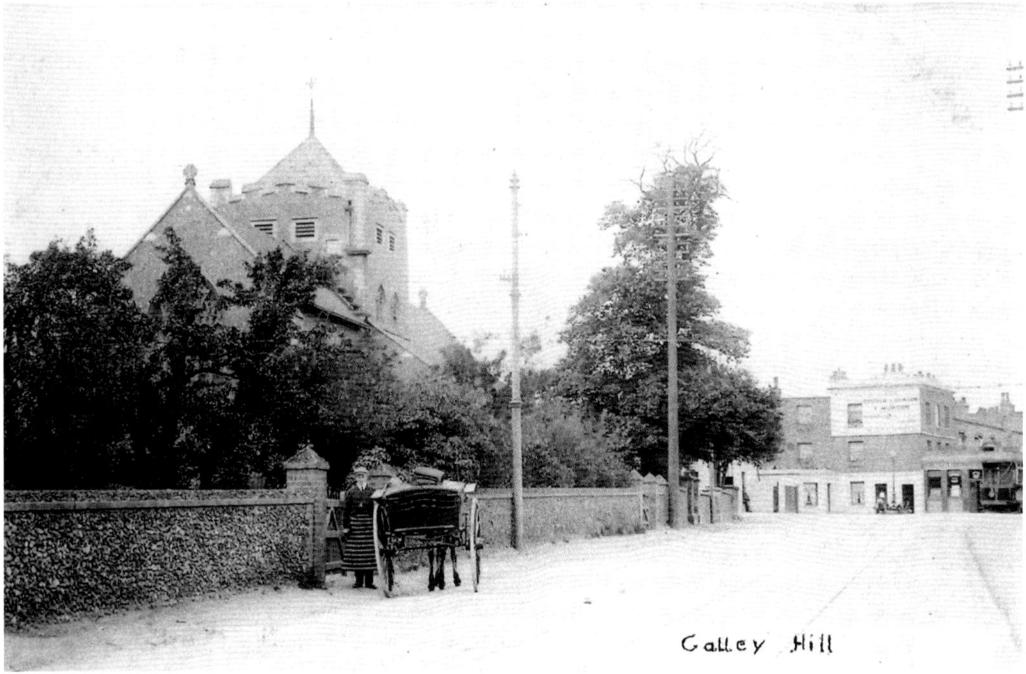

7. Galley Hill looking west, circa 1910. The scene is looking towards the George & Dragon public house, which is clearly seen on the corner with High Street. A Gravesend tramcar has stopped outside of the George & Dragon. Public transport has always used this as a stop as it does today – the tram conductors shouting 'Holy City' when arriving at Swanscombe. The meaning of calling Swanscombe 'holy' was probably a pun on 'holey', in that chalk pits surrounded the town. The tram system existed from 1902 to 1929, but one thing, which has had a revival in today's world, is shopping delivery. Here is the cart of a local tradesman delivering to the wealthier houses of Galley Hill.

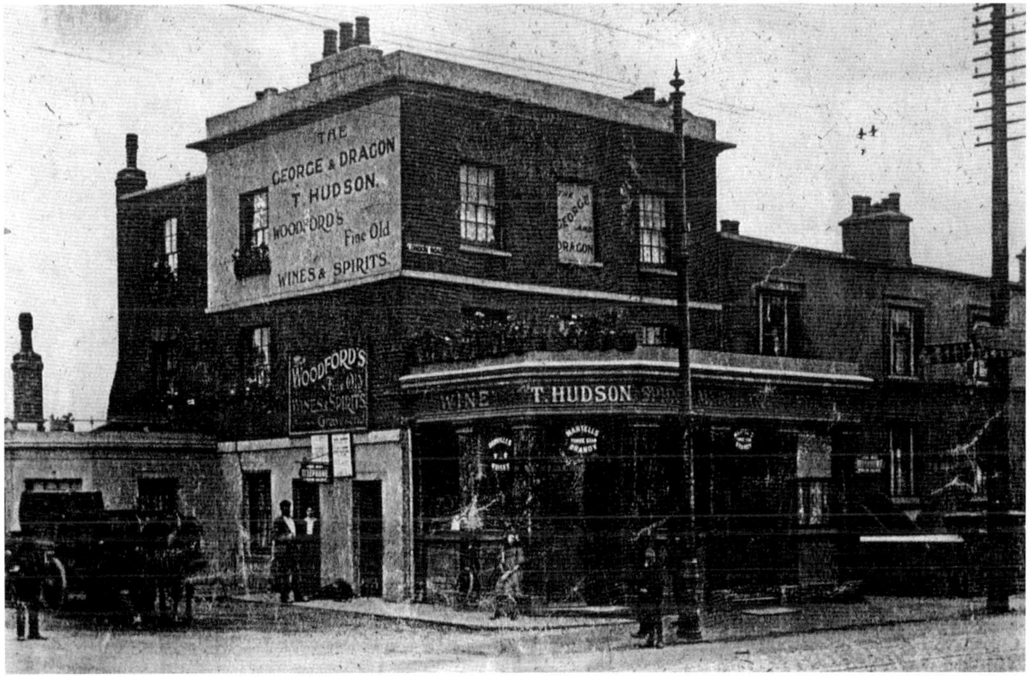

8. The George & Dragon public house, Galley Hill circa 1912. The George & Dragon was one of Swanscombe's major pubs and was able to provide spirits, accommodation and stabling in addition to beer. It stands on the main Strood to Dartford turnpike road; this section was turnpiked in 1738. The present building is believed to date from the 1840s but an earlier house existed to pick up the passing road trade. Until the 1840s Galley Hill was a hamlet physically separate from Swanscombe itself (which was along Swanscombe Street), but massive growth caused by cement workers' housing, caused Galley Hill to merge with the rest of Swanscombe. Note the terraced buildings next to the pub – these were redeveloped in the late 1970s into industrial units. The landlord listed is Thomas Hudson who ran the business from 1897 to 1914.

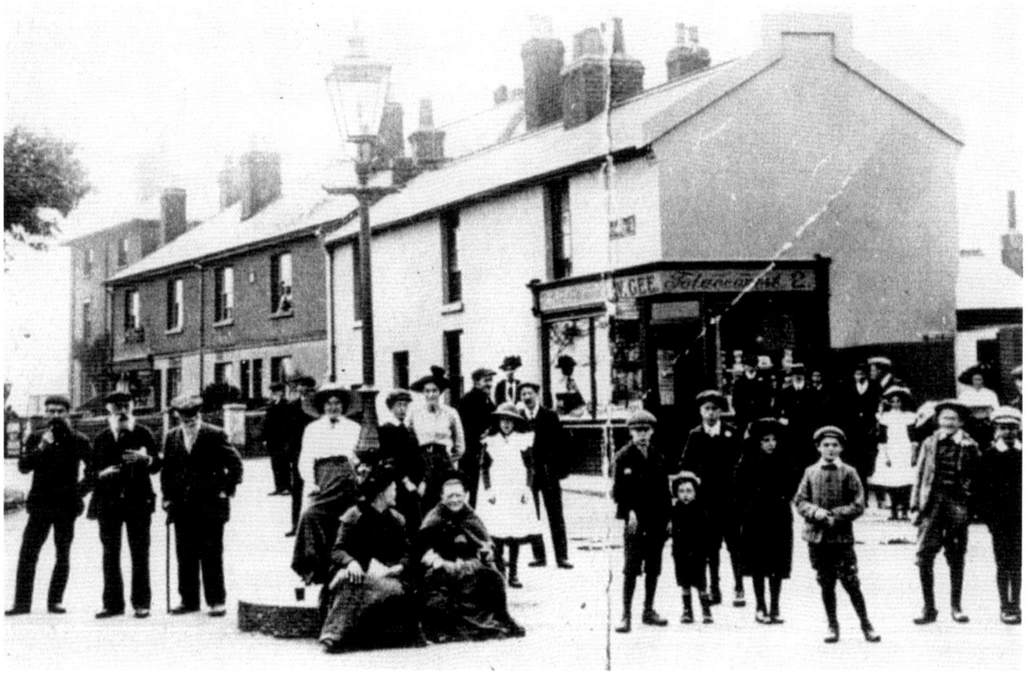

9. Gee's Tobacconists, High Street. This view is on the west side of the High Street near the George & Dragon. Most of the buildings dated from the 1850-1880 period, when the previously largely empty road grew rapidly with the cement workers' influx. Gee's shop was in operation from about 1912 to the 1950s, later selling sweets as well as tobacco. Hot cordials were provided at the shop for tram drivers in winter. These were prepared in the private apartment on the range with a black kettle. Sweets displayed in the window were in dishes with little paper doyleys. The Gee family themselves only allowed their children to eat boiled sweets, which were considered safe from diseases such as diphtheria.

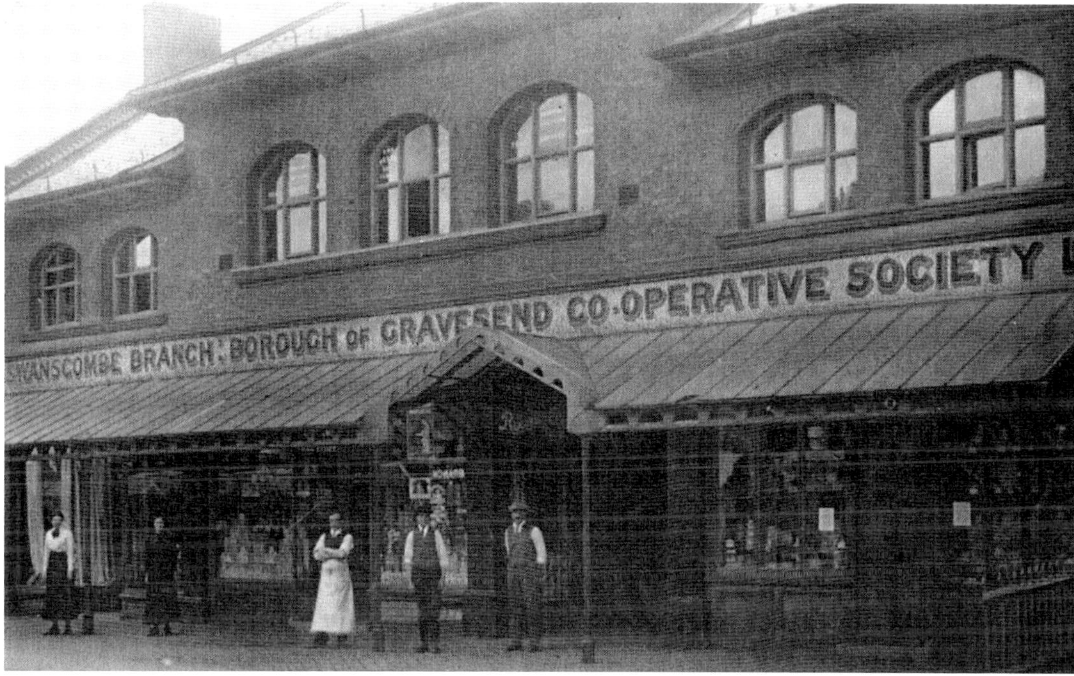

10. Co-Operative Society Shops, High Street. This view was taken around 1914 – the parade was opened in 1913. The 'CO-OP' symbolised the working class ideals of self help and it also shows that Swanscombe felt greater affinity with Gravesend and Northfleet rather than Dartford – if for no other reason than the trams ran direct to Gravesend. The Gravesend Co-Operative Society began its Swanscombe branch in about 1889 – it was in operation by 1891 – William John Francis then being the manager when it was situated in Broomfield Road. This building dominated (and still does) the upper part of the High Street in Galley Hill and contained (in 1937) a grocers, drapers and outfitters and a butcher in addition to halls above used by numerous community groups and for wedding receptions. This building replaced two thatched cottages, which had burned down earlier. The Co-Operative movement in Gravesend ceased in the 1980s, since when this building has been used by different shops.

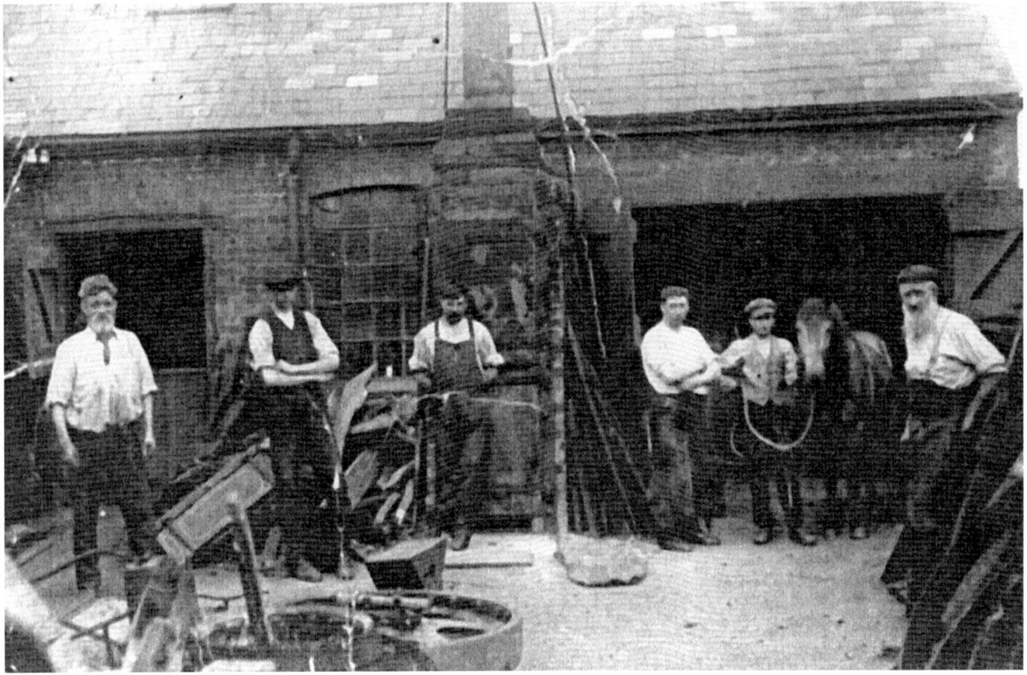

11. The Forge, High Street. The garage of its time, the forge not only shoed horses but made and repaired almost any metalwork object. The forge shown here was a product of the industrial rather than the agricultural period, as its position in the High Street would have been an empty country lane until the 1850s. The forge was operated by Messrs. Bundy and Williams at the turn of the twentieth century and consisted of a yard, a building directly on the High Street and the smithy itself behind at the rear of the site. The forge had adapted to the end of the horse age by becoming the 'Old Forge Garages' where it repaired cars by the late 1930s. In 1938 the site was worked by Messrs. F. Axford and J.D. Love, who operated the garage, while Pearce Brothers, who were corn and seed merchants, also occupied the area. During the 1960s the whole site was redeveloped as an ugly new post office which itself became Swanscombe Dry Cleaners during the mid-1980s.

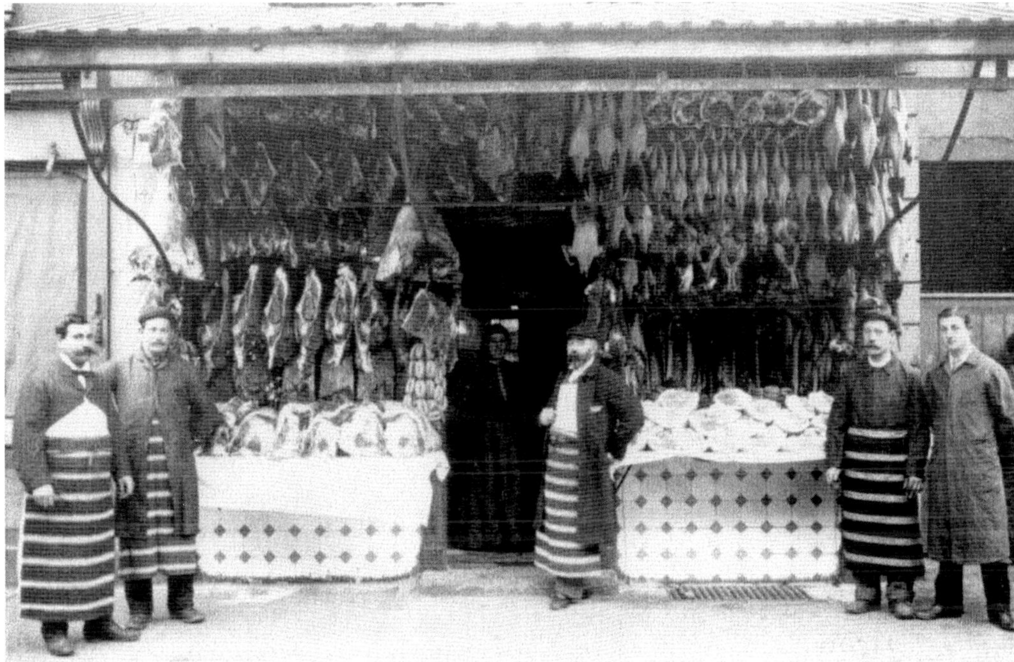

12. Bond's Butcher Shop, High Street. A typical feature of any town or village was the butcher's shop. In the days before refrigeration the meat was displayed in the open air and if unsold during the day it would be often sold off very cheap or given away very late at night. Poorer families would wait until such times in order to obtain occasional meat in their diet. Like most shops, Bonds would slaughter their own stock with the resultant screams and rivers of blood in a densely populated area. A strange homemade flywheel sausage machine existed at the rear of the shop operated by both petrol and gas in the mid-1920s. Bonds operated from the premises at 62 High Street from about 1892 until 1918, then at 108 High Street until about 1921. Bonds also had another butcher's shop in Milton Road.

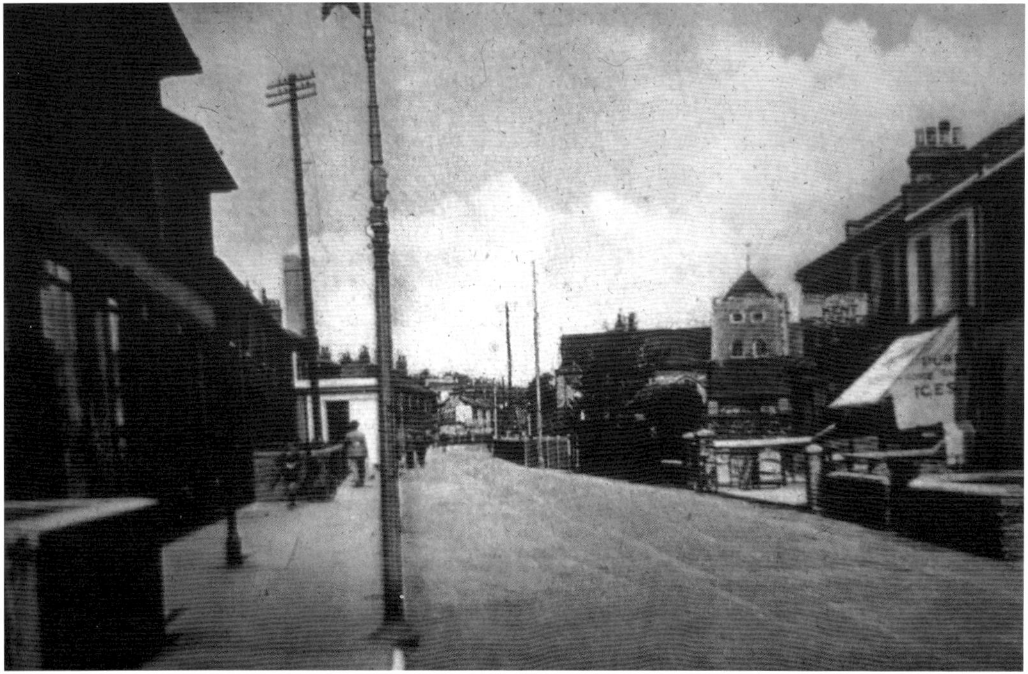

13. High Street, Swanscombe circa 1935. A view looking north. In the background can be seen the ubiquitous cement factory chimney belching out the bane of the housewife – cement dust settled on washing as well as roofs and gardens. Swanscombe was still very self-contained despite bus and rail connections to elsewhere. The Kent Messenger shop shown (the proprietor was L.G. Peacock) was well used by the few people who commuted to London – most locals worked in or around Swanscombe in the 1930s. Further down on the right was Albert Banks' Cycle Shop, which sold motorcycles and wirelesses (radios). It was a shop for recharging accumulators (heavy batteries used for powering electrical equipment) and car batteries could also be topped up from here. Behind All Saint's Church was its parish room, a wooden hut used by various clubs including one of the 'Slate Clubs', which meant weekly subscriptions of a few pennies, to build a fund for medical insurance in the days prior to the National Health Service.

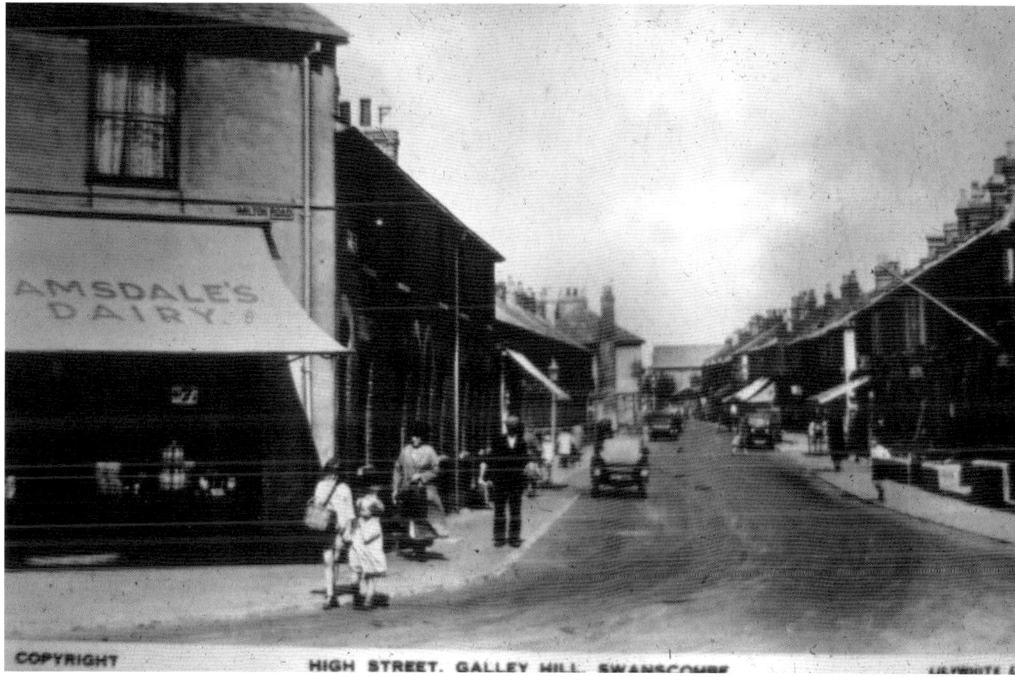

14. High Street, Galley Hill, circa 1938. View looking north. The Galley Hill name still continued, even though this had long been considered Swanscombe High Street. The area was bristling with businesses in shops, which were often converted terraced houses. The pole on the right marks the barbershop of Frederick Homewood at this time. By looking at a local street directory in the late 1930s this one road had the following businesses: a tobacconist, confectioner, baker, co-operative society, two pubs, a general store, cycles, hairdressers, post office, printer, fishmonger and fish and chips, greengrocer, clothier, butcher, boot maker, corn and seed merchant, garage, laundry, hardware, chemist, optician, photographer and draper; several of these businesses had two different shops in the High Street alone.

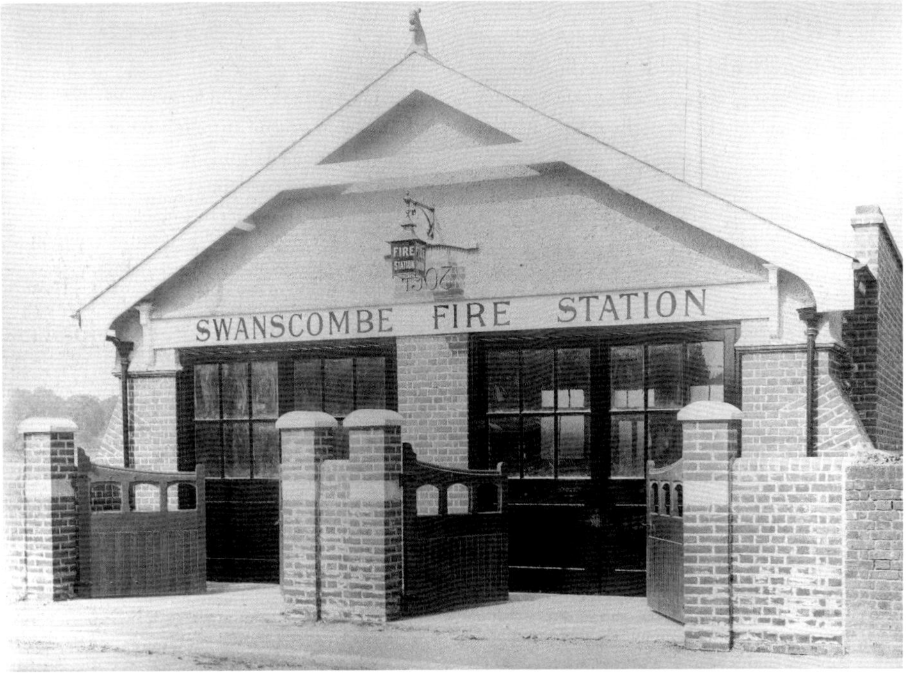

15. Swanscombe Fire Station, 1908. It was with great civic pride that the fire station in Church Road was officially opened on Saturday, 13 June 1908. Swanscombe Parish Council had been very keen to establish a properly organised fire service in the 1890s and by 1898-1899 a temporary fire station had been established at Galley Hill (in addition to one at Greenhithe). In 1907 land at the south end of the Primitive Methodist Chapel was for sale and purchased by Swanscombe Parish Council. In November 1907 plans were drawn up for a new fire station and proposals for a first floor with council chamber were dropped, to be taken up again in the 1920s. The opening day saw a parade of neighbouring fire brigades from Gravesend, Northfleet, Crayford, Dartford, Horton Kirby, Longfield and other places. The fire engines were led by Swanscombe's Captain A.E. Kent (1872-1940) and preceded by the band of the training ship 'Arethusa'. The church bells were ringing, flags out and a huge crowd assembled in the streets – a wonderful contemporary example of Swanscombe's pride in its civic achievements.

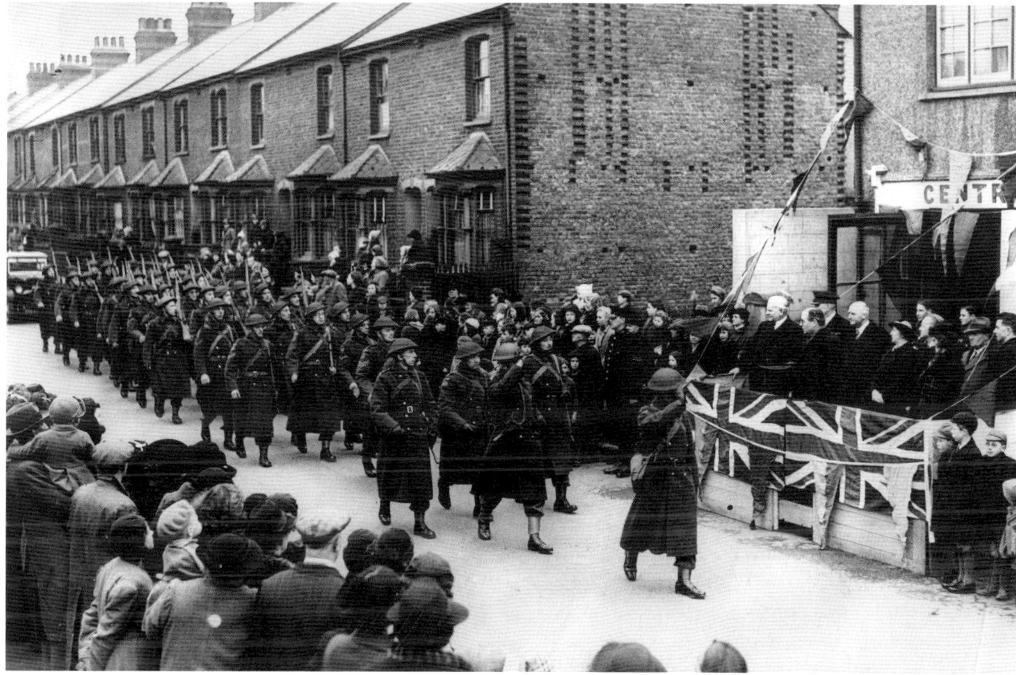

16. March past of Swanscombe Home Guard, Church Road, 3 December 1944. This is the 'B' company of the 17th Battalion of the Kent Home Guard, which covered Swanscombe. The Home Guard began in 1939 and was originally the Local Defence Volunteers, who only had two rifles between them. The Home Guard met at the Methodist Chapel in Church Road (later the Scouts Headquarters) but soon transferred to Galley Hill School on London Road for their headquarters. There were two patrols at night consisting of three men each (usually two older men and one young lad who was the runner of messages) that patrolled Swanscombe. Drilling, exercises and combat training also took place on the football ground within the Recreation Ground. The march past was a morale boost for all and taking the salute outside the fire station (later the library) are members of Swanscombe Urban District Council. This was the official stand down of the Swanscombe Home Guard. Note on the right the terraced houses with brick marks – this terrace was to have been extended until Swanscombe Parish Council purchased the land for the fire station in 1907.

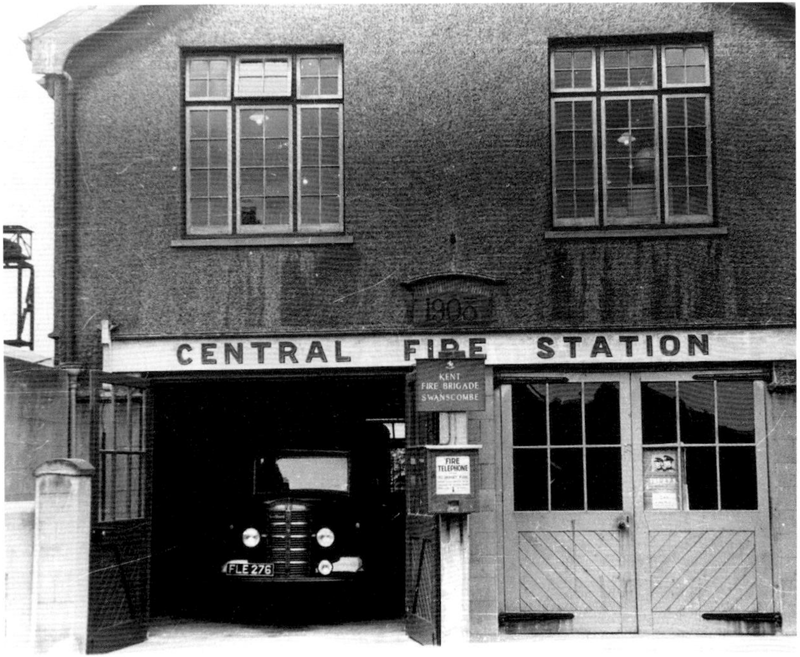

17. Swanscombe Central Fire Station and Swanscombe Library, circa 1949. The building shown here still remains in Church Road. Swanscombe Urban District Council operated the fire brigade until 1941, when the National Fire Service was set up in response to the Second World War. In 1948 Kent County Council became responsible for the county's fire brigades – the vehicle seen here is a modified Bedford lorry, which was a utility fire engine created at the beginning of the Second World War. Swanscombe Branch Library occupied the upper floor of the building from 1928 until moving down to the ground floor in 1968. The upper floor was added to the single storey fire station in 1922 as a council chamber but vacated by Swanscombe Council in 1926. The entrance to the library was along the alleyway on the left side of the building and then via a back door and flight of wooden stairs. Swanscombe was a pioneer of the Kent County Library system, which operated in those Kentish communities that did not provide their own public library service. Conditions were primitive with only gaslights at first, no toilet and no running water. Swanscombe Library remained in this building from November 1928 until November 2002, when it was removed to Swan Valley School. Until its move, the library was the oldest small branch in Kent to still remain in its original building.

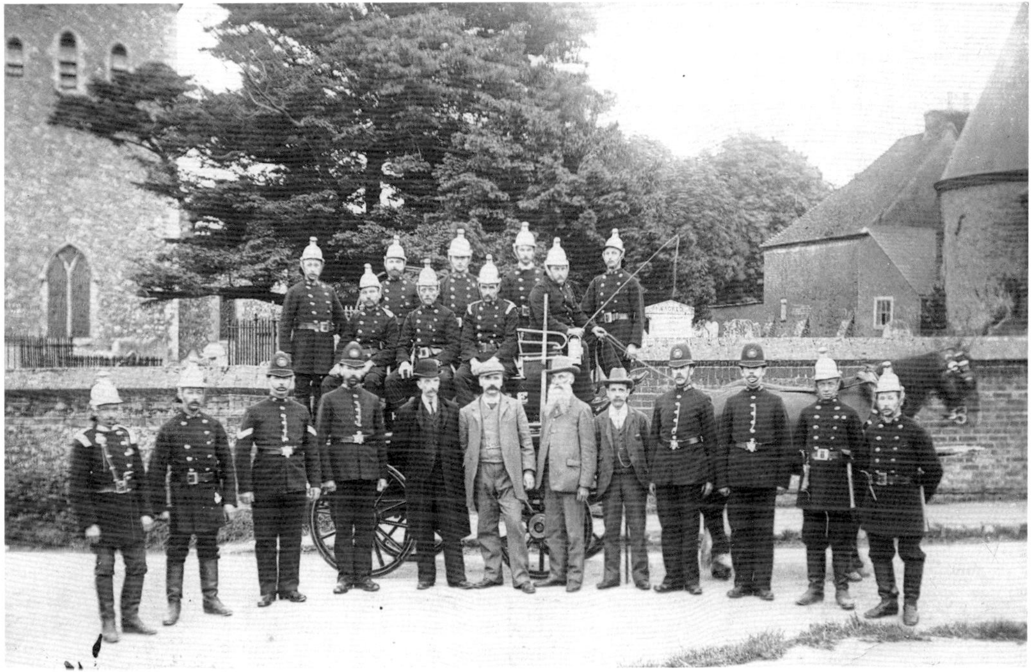

18. Swanscombe Parish Fire Brigade outside Saint Peter and Pauls' Church. Shortly after the foundation of Swanscombe Parish Council in 1894, the urgent need for an organised fire fighting force occupied the minds of the councillors. On 4 October 1898 the council decided to form a fire brigade with two stations (at Swanscombe and Greenhithe), five men at each station and all under one captain. The well-established Northfleet Fire Brigade was asked for advice and they recommended a total of £88 18/- be spent on equipment including two hose carts, six scaling ladders, various lengths of hose and ten uniforms. Three extra water hydrants were recommended and because all the existing hydrants had different sized hose couplings, making them useless for fire fighting, it was recommended that they all be one size! The picture shows the horse-drawn manual fire engine which replaced the hose carts shortly after 1903 and was itself replaced by a motorised engine during the inter war years. The hose carts were so heavy to manoeuvre that the firemen were exhausted by the time they actually reached a fire.

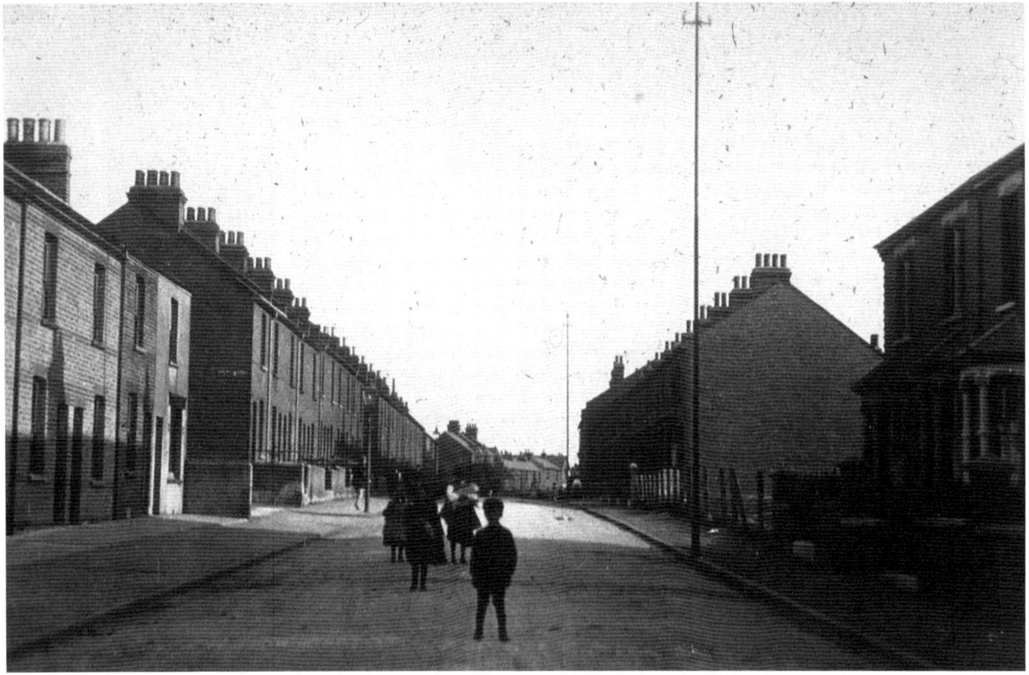

19. Church Road, Swanscombe circa 1905. Church Road follows the line of an old footpath, which ran parallel to Stanhope Road linking the Galley Hill area with Swanscombe Village itself. Most of Church Road ran through fields and past hedgerows until the 1880s – only a few cottages and a small brewery and beer house, which was the original Morning Star public house, existed here before. This view shows Church Road before it was fully developed with housing – note the gas lamp-post and cottages on the left with no front gardens. Further up on the left, and the houses on the right, do have small gardens and these features give an indication of the respective rents and therefore the social mix of the tenants.
The gap on the left is Harmer Road with its school opened in 1893, closed in 1967 and then used as a youth club before demolition in November 1998. Many of the gaps seen on the right side were filled with housing in the 1920s and 1930s.

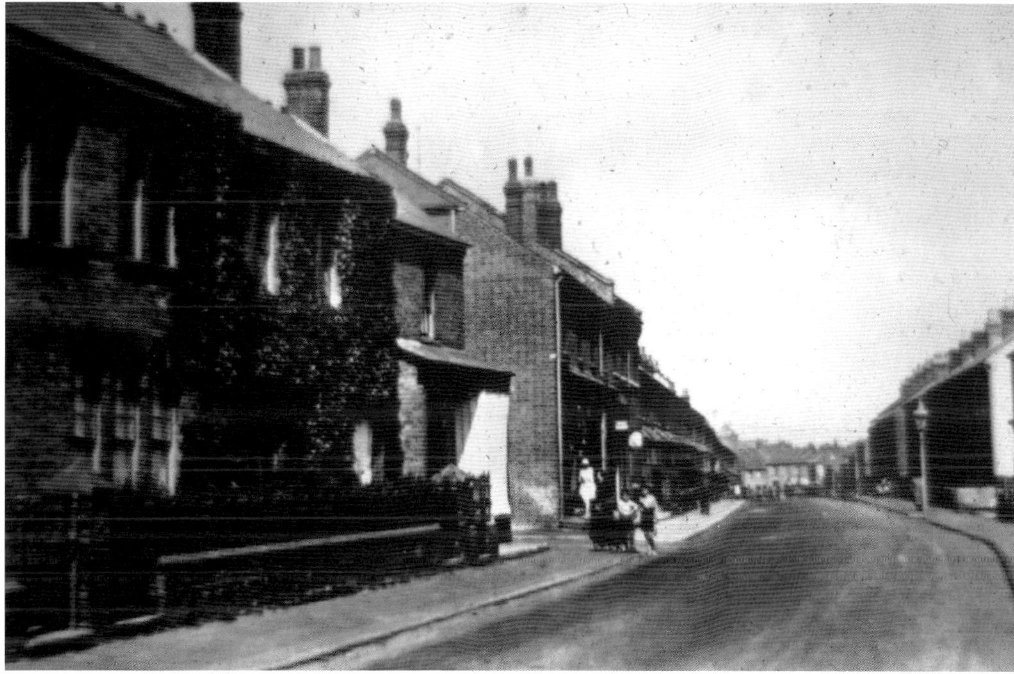

20. Church Road, Swanscombe circa 1935. Church Road has been so called since the 1890s. Previously it had several names – originally known as Bird's Row and in the 1881 census it was called Barnfield Road, not becoming Church Road until after the Methodist chapel was built in 1888. In 1890 sale particulars list properties in Birds Row including a baker's shop (with parlour, kitchen scullery, four bedrooms and bakehouse with 10 bushel oven and storage over the top), and Ivy Cottage complete with coach house and stable. The road developed in a piece meal fashion. An example was in 1911 when local builder F.W. Ramsay built two terraced houses for William Jenns at a cost of £349 4/-, these were numbers 8 and 10 Church Road, while seven cottages built between 105 and 117 Church Road were constructed in the 1920s by Sargeants – a Northfleet builder. Even this view displays various styles and ages of housing showing the haphazard way it was developed.

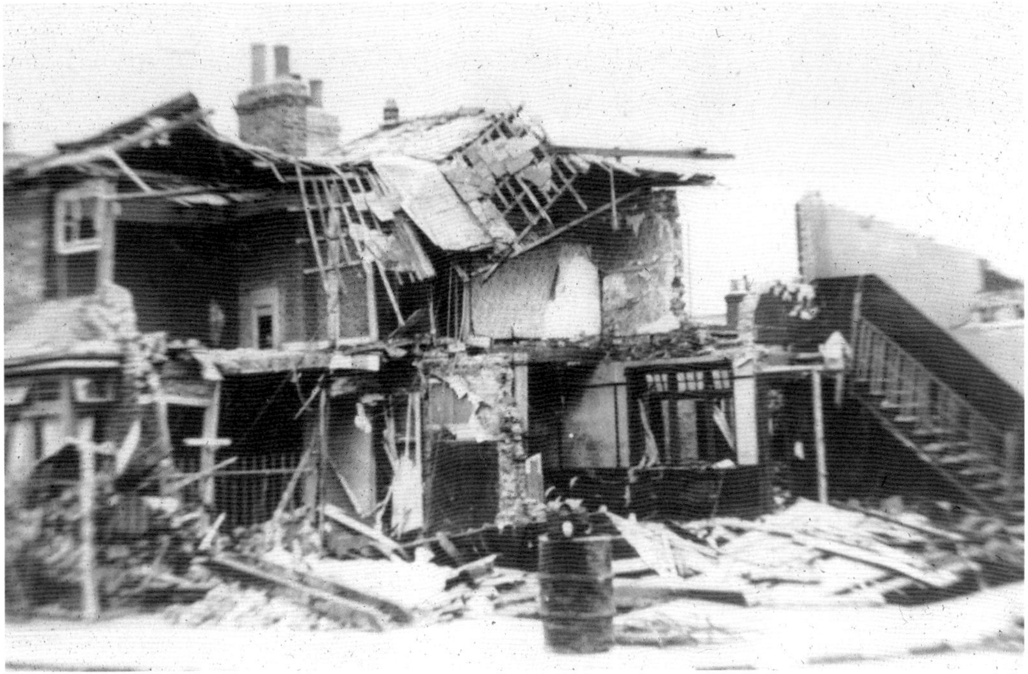

21. Morning Star public house, Church Road. The earliest mentions of the pub were in the 1750s when it was a beer house in Bird's Row (later Church Road). The building was rebuilt about 1890 and in the 1930s was tenanted by Russell's Brewery of Gravesend to Frederick Oram who was also landlord of the Coopers Arms in Craylands Lane. In 1938 and 1939 the pub's tenant was Archie Edward Stevens but on 10th November 1940, 27 people were killed including the landlord when the pub received a direct hit from a stray bomb just after 8 p.m. A temporary wooden building, which made the beer warm in summer and which had no toilets, replaced it. The present building was opened in 1960 but it caused a stir in Swanscombe as it had different prices in the saloon and public bars.

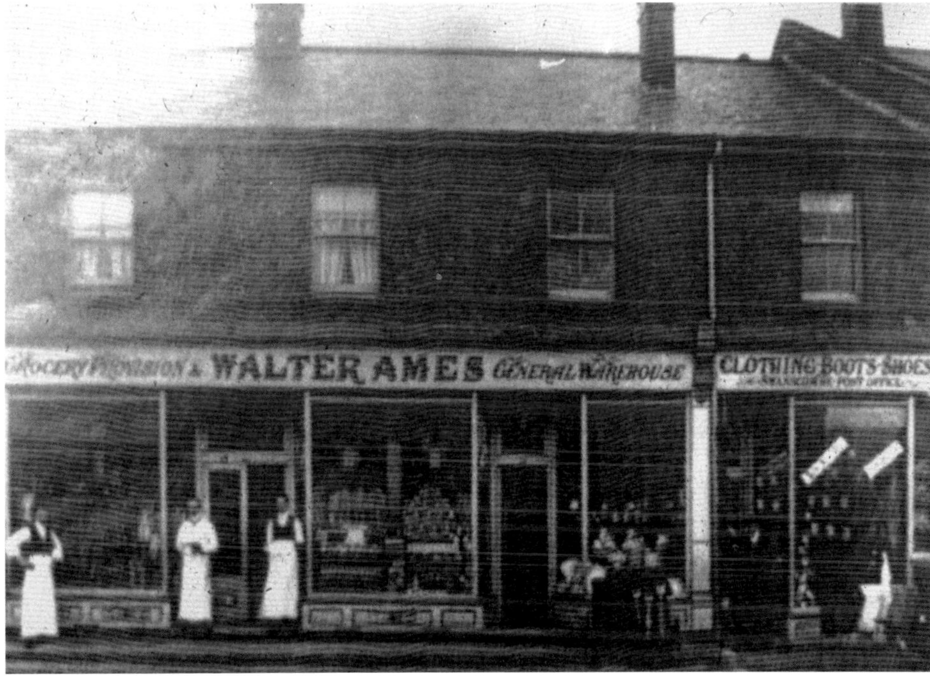

22. Walter Ames' shops, Church Road circa 1920. Walter Ames was a leading light in Swanscombe's civic as well as its economic affairs. By 1907 Ames had already established a considerable business empire, and by 1937 it covered the premises 88-98 Church Road. Ames was a boot and shoe dealer, clothier, draper, general warehouse, grocer and he ran Church Road post office. In his early years he is also listed as a baker. In 1894, when Swanscombe Parish Council was established, Walter Ames became its first chairman, an honour repeated in 1926 when he was the first chairman of the new Swanscombe Urban District Council. Ames was described as short with a well-groomed beard. He was well liked, very well known and seen as a man of action. Ames died in 1934 and was described as the 'Father of Swanscombe Council'.

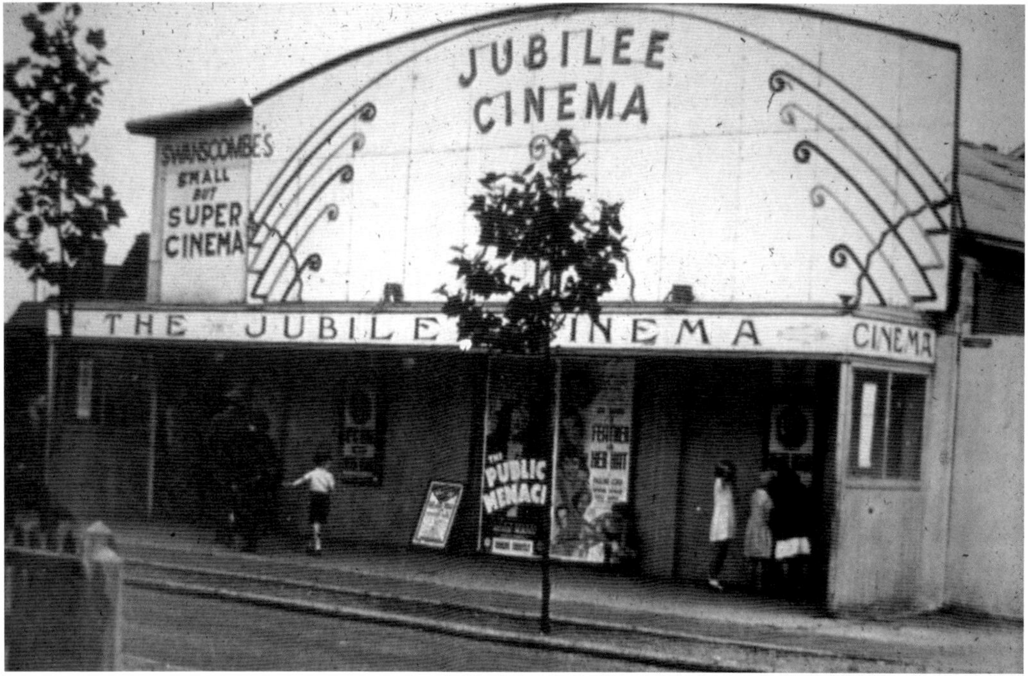

23. Jubilee Cinema, Ames Road, 1935. In 1923 the cinema brought the world of films and the images of the age via newsreels to Swanscombe as the Electric Cinema. In 1935 it became the Jubilee Cinema and it was owned by local councillor and grocer Mr. Charles Mercer, who combined the businesses of entertainment and grocery by having a shack next to the cinema before moving his grocery business to Milton Road. Mercer died in 1943, having lost money on his cinema venture. In typical Swanscombe style the cinema seats were back to front (i.e. the seats faced you at the entrance and the screen was at the front instead of the back of the building). Similarly the expensive seats in Swanscombe were at the front and the cheap seats (with the better view) were at the back. This was so because the sound system was so dreadful only the front seats with the poorer view could hear the film. Nobody could hear the sound when it rained because of the din made on the corrugated iron roof. Children's films shown on Saturdays were known as the Saturday Afternoon Crush and the whole cinema was called the 'Bug Hutch' because of its condition. In 1939 it was reconstructed as the Wardona and demolished in 1958.

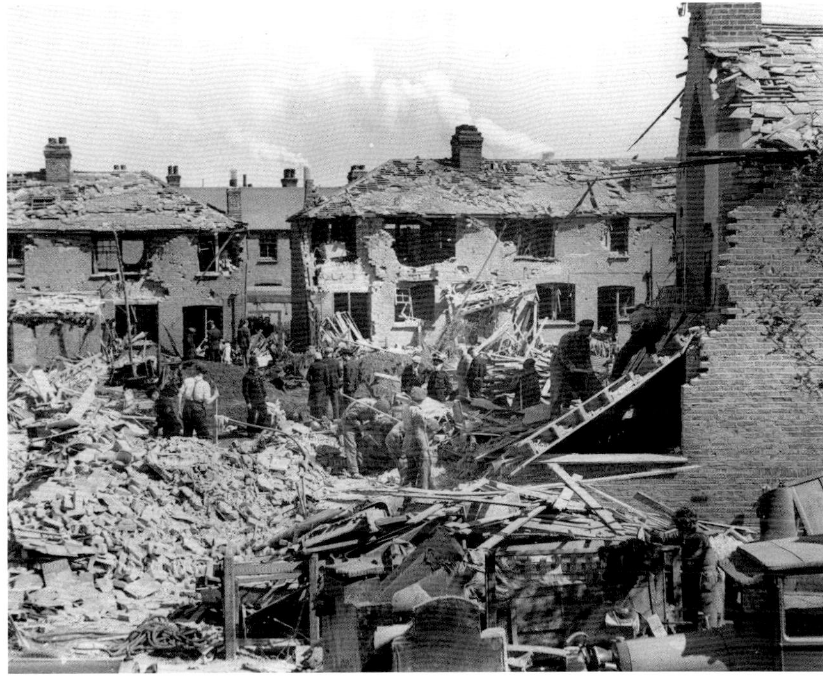

24. Bomb damage: Ames Road and Lewis Road. A photograph showing high explosive bomb damage the bombs being dropped at 1.19 a.m. on 18th May 1943. Raids such as this created huge logistical problems for Swanscombe Urban District Council in rehousing families and clearing debris to make roads passable. The houses shown here were model dwellings built by the council: Ames Road in the late 1920s and Lewis Road in the 1930s. Apparently two small boys were blown onto a roof by the blast suffering only minor injuries.

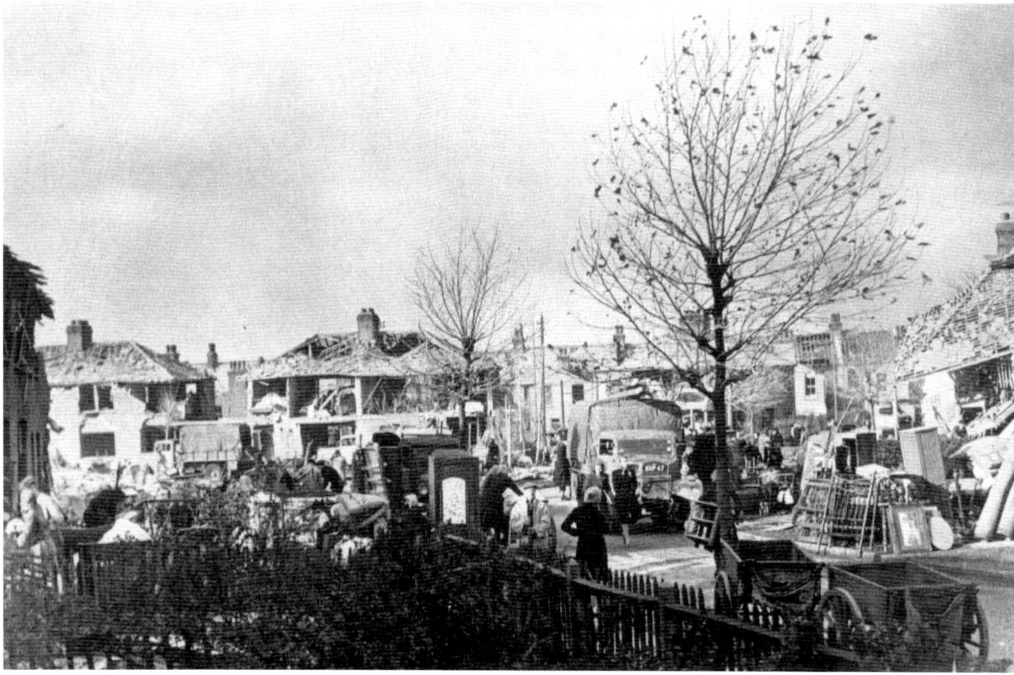

25. Bomb damage in Trebble Road and Ames Road. Another view of one of Swanscombe's many bombing incidents during the Second World War. The view shows Ames Road joining Trebble Road after a raid in early November 1944. Despite the damage only one person was killed with eight more in hospital and 21 needing first aid. The actual damage caused six houses to be totally destroyed with seven more having to be demolished. Some eighty people were sent to a rest centre and Swanscombe was very well organised in dealing with vast amounts of damage. This incident was caused by a V1 flying bomb.

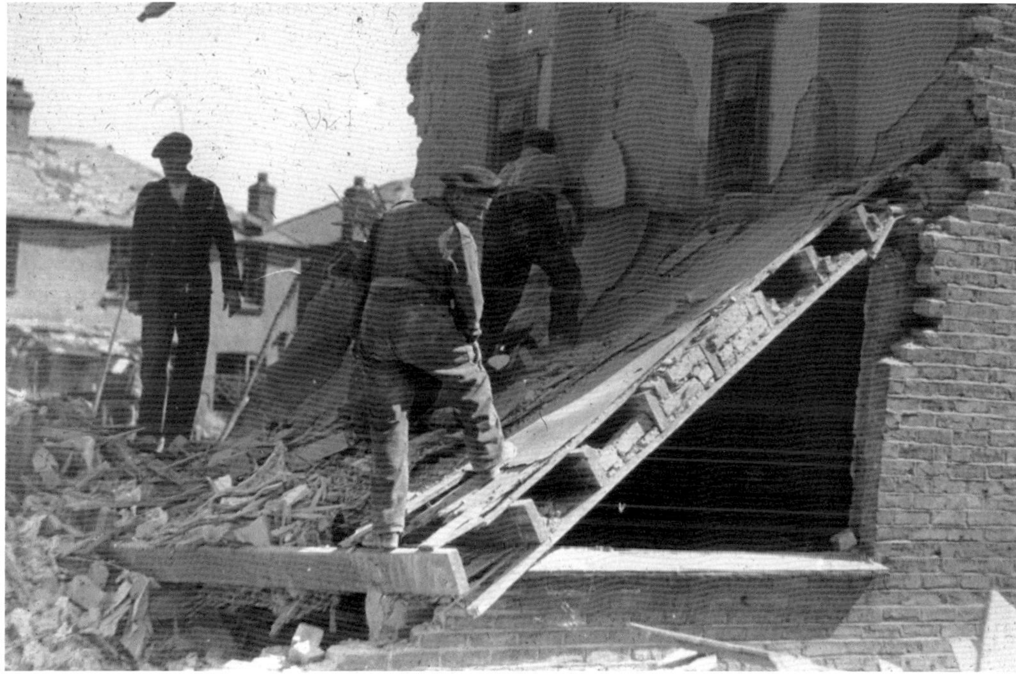

26. Air raid damage in Broad Road. This view is of the damage caused on 7 August 1944 when a V1 (flying bomb) destroyed four houses because it fell short of its intended destination of London. The emergency services and Swanscombe Urban District Council then had to rehouse 48 families, treating the injured and making the area safe from collapsing buildings and any unexploded bombs. The photograph shows an example of how the ground floor of the houses was filled with the rubble from the bedrooms and roof and also the Victorian iron fire places, which were rarely used to heat the bedrooms because of the cost of fuel.

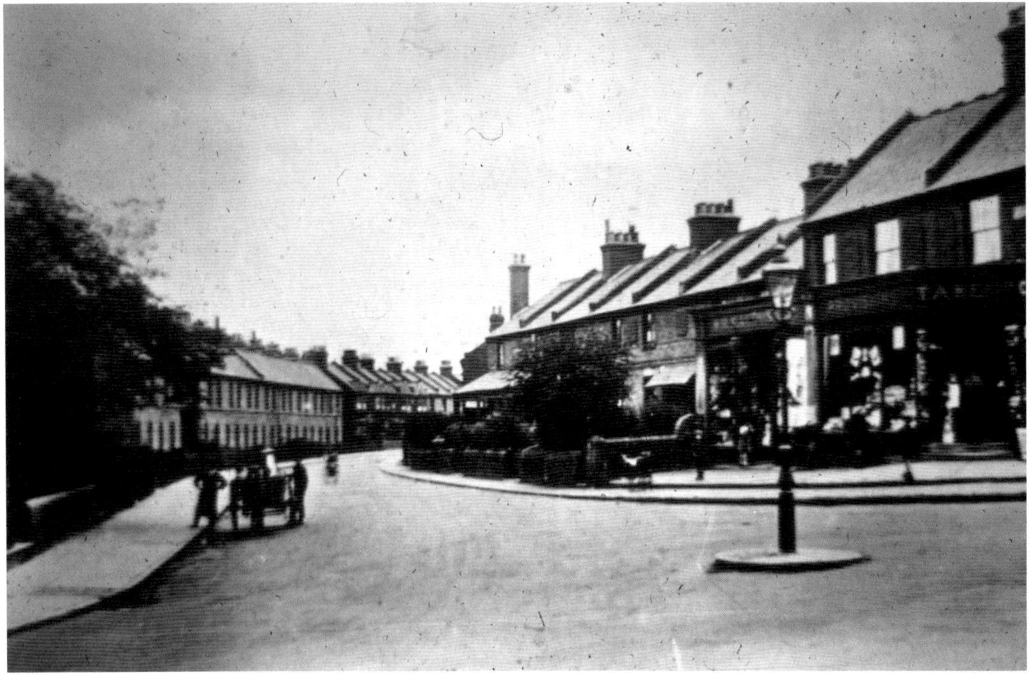

27. Stanhope Road, Swanscombe circa 1930. The junction of Stanhope Road and the High Street as it was around 1930. It was then known as 'Kemp's Corner' as Kemp's grocery shop was directly on the junction. Macdonald's draper's shop then joined the buildings around into Stanhope Road itself. The houses on the left were known locally as 'The Slabs' and also as 'Squint Eye Row' on account of the front parlours being different shapes in each house so as to fit on the building plots as the road bent around the corner. As this area was often considered the centre of Swanscombe, the lamp-post in the picture was used to greet the New Year at midnight on 31 December, by people singing and socialising.

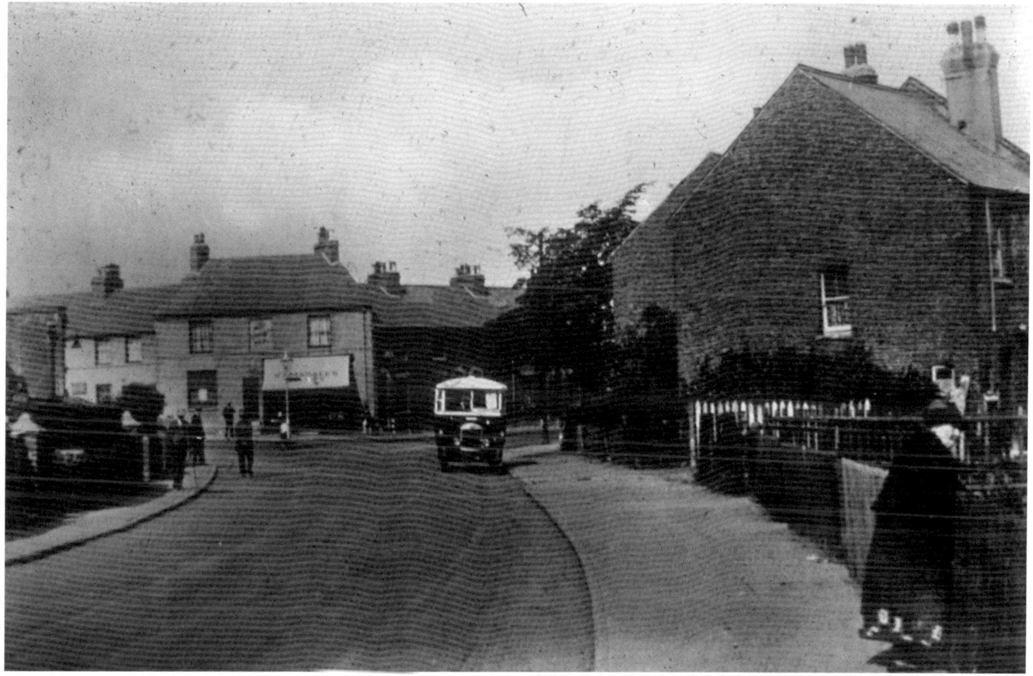

28. 'The Square', Swanscombe. Everyone who knows Swanscombe is aware that there has never been an area known as 'The Square'. The view is the junction of Stanhope Road into the High Street around 1935. The bus service had replaced the trams in 1929 and, unlike the trams, the buses had flexible routes down into Swanscombe itself instead of by passing the town along London Road which was the case with the trams. The Slabs or 'Squint Eye Row' cottages can be seen on the right of the picture, but it is Ramsdales Dairy, which dominated the view at this time. The dairy was formerly 'The Prince of Wales' public house, which ceased business around 1914 becoming one of the three dairies in Swanscombe, which survived into the late 1930s. The whole parade of shops including Ramsdale's Dairy and the neighbouring cottages in Milton Road (to the left) were demolished in 1961 and replaced by a red brick row of shops. This later development was designed to improve Swanscombe's shopping and made a major visual impact in an area of Victorian development.

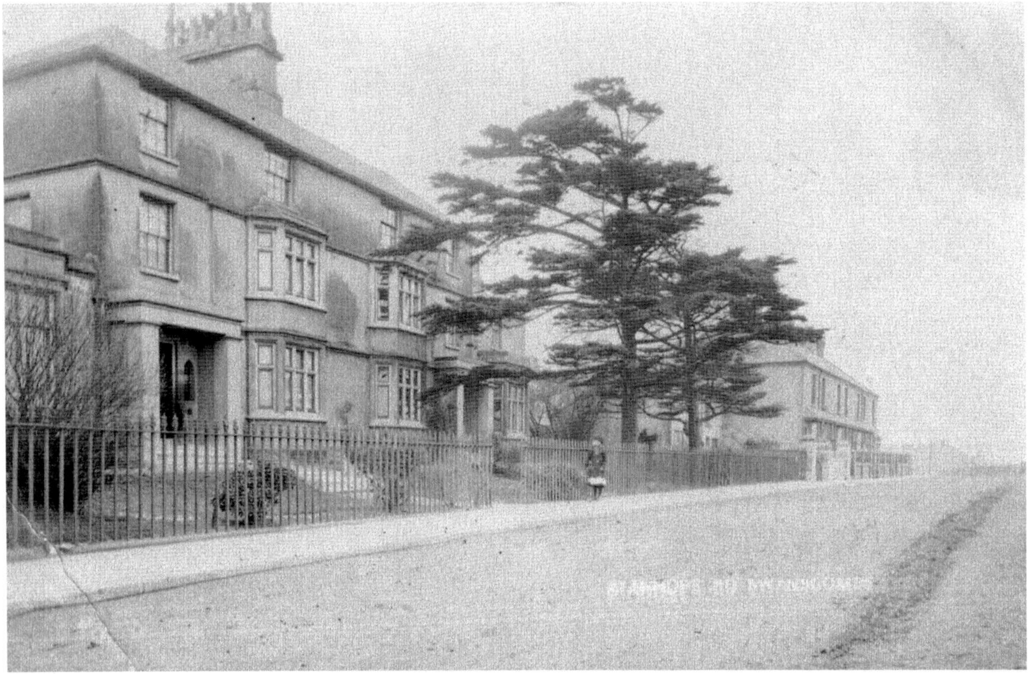

29. Belle Vue House, Stanhope Road circa 1910. This house is unlike the workers cottages, which were rapidly covering Swanscombe from the 1840s onwards. Belle Vue was situated with views over the Ebbsfleet Valley towards Northfleet prior to the excavation of the land and before industrialisation had covered the area. The sales particulars of a very similar building on Galley Hill show us that there was a handsome entrance hall with kitchens, wine cellar and coal cellar in the basement. The ground floor having two parlours with a water closet and a handsome staircase to the next floor with two good chambers: one front and one back complete with a neat dressing room with two roomy chambers on the top floor. A coach house with loft over came as part of the property as did gardens and the house was newly constructed in 1846. Swanscombe Urban District councillor Thomas Kemp lived here until the mid-1930s. During the Second World War the house was used as flats for bombed-out families and it has been a home for the elderly since the 1980s. During the interwar years the house next door was the home and practice of Dr. Michael Lynch, one of three general practitioners in Swanscombe at that time.

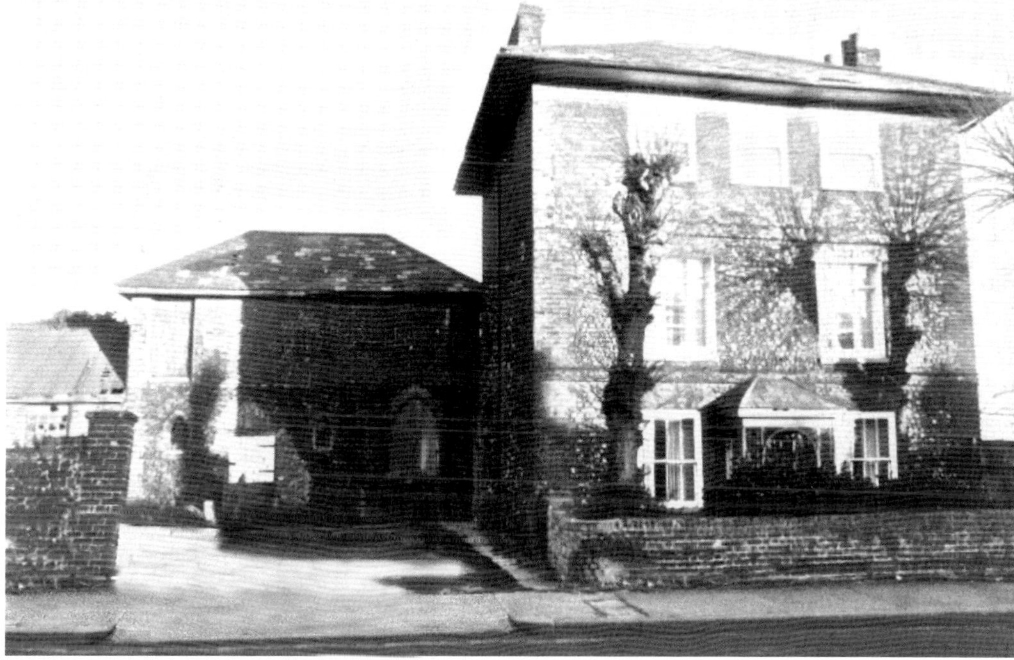

30. Rixson's Farm, Stanhope Road. This farmhouse was known as 'Lodge Farm' during the twentieth century and as 'Swanscombe Lodge' in the nineteenth century. The house contained much flint in addition to brickwork and probably dated from the eighteenth century before being altered in Victorian times. The farm occupied much of the land between Stanhope Road and the border with Northfleet, and was in the ownership of Mr. S.C. Umfreville of Ingress Abbey during the 1870s. William Rixson later occupied the farm, before he gave up the site in 1944. Lodge Farm had acres of orchards in the nineteenth century but its fields were steadily taken over as allotments so that Swanscombe locals could access extra food for themselves and by 1938 the rest of the farmland had been destroyed by chalk quarrying. The house was still able to sell some produce but soon became dilapidated. The farm was eventually demolished in 1984.

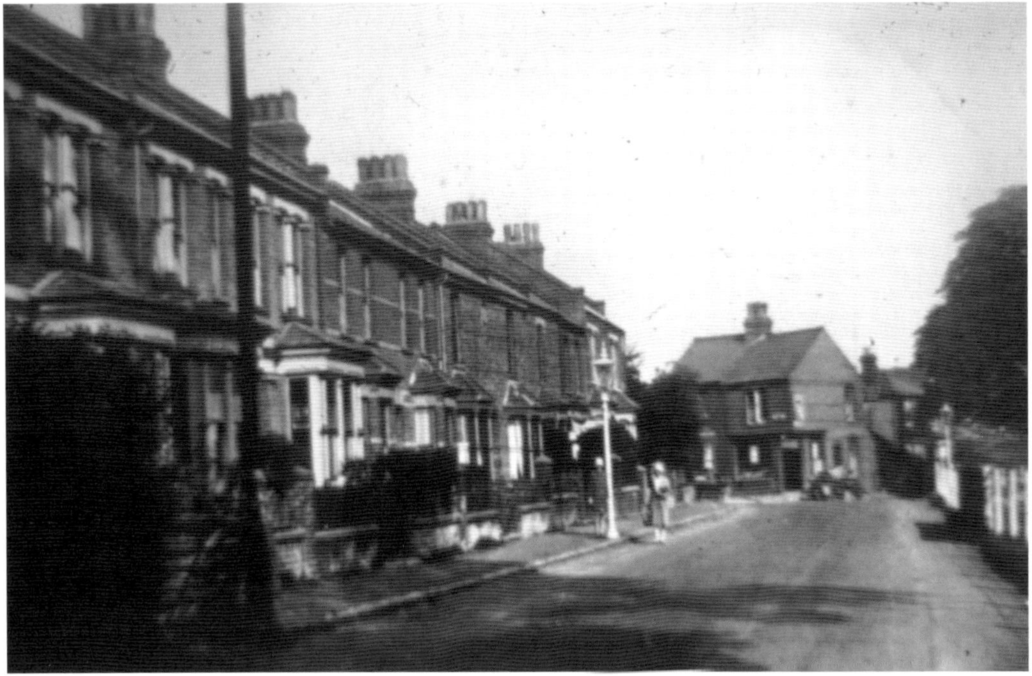

31. Southfleet Road, Swanscombe circa 1930. The view shows the twelve properties built after the sale of the land along the western edge of Southfleet Road in 1891. Originally a row of some 32 houses and shops was to occupy a great length of the road but most were never constructed. The Swan Valley School grounds occupy the site of the un-built houses but this small row had one shop in it: W.J. Pring, which was a general shop also selling sweets. The locals of the 1930s would wander down Southfleet Road to look at the newly-constructed 3-lane A2 and see the traffic on a Sunday night. Mr. Pring's shop was one of the few businesses open on a Sunday night to supply the needs of local traffic spotting: a custom that has long since lost its appeal in this age of almost universal car ownership.

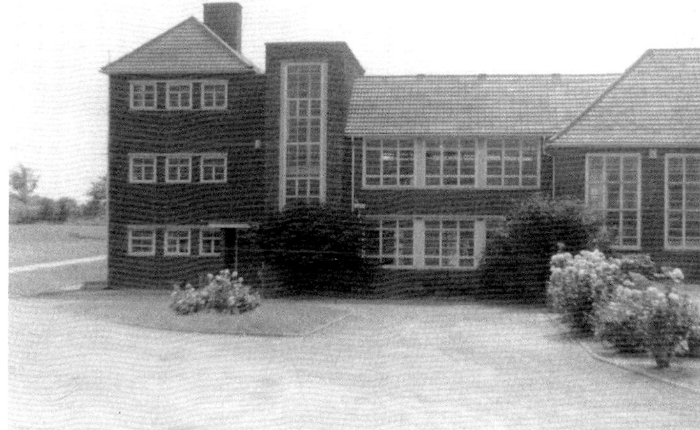

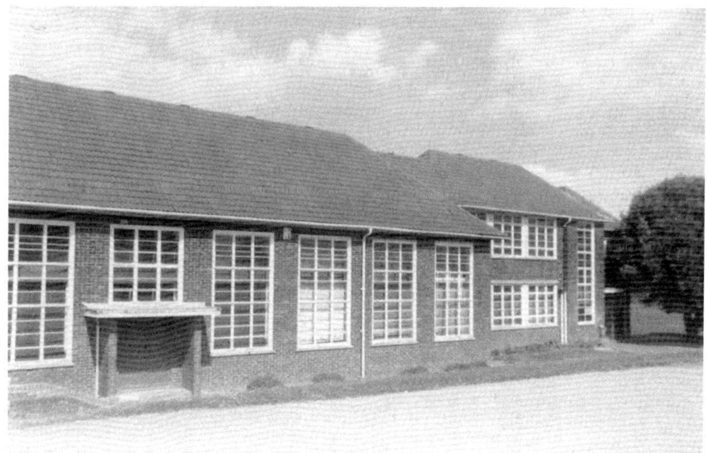

32. Swanscombe Secondary School, Southfleet Road. The school had a very colourful history. It began in 1938 as a junior girls and infants in temporary buildings behind terraced houses in Southfleet Road. The site was originally part of the Mansion House estate and included orchards and a hop garden of some 15 acres. During the Second World War the new building was not used as a school because the huge glass windows were considered too dangerous if broken in air raids. After 1945 the school was extended and enlarged – it became the Swanscombe Secondary School for both sexes by 1967 and continued until 1992, when it was decided to close the school, demolish the buildings and scatter Swanscombe's considerable secondary school aged pupils to surrounding areas. The stupidity of this political move was clearly demonstrated when a new secondary school was then built on the site in 1998 being the first in the area for twenty years. The new school was called 'Swan Valley Community School' and was constructed under the controversial 'Private Finance Initiative' system of funding – the results of which future generations will inherit. In November 2002 Swanscombe's old branch library in Church Road closed and moved to a new ccommodation within this new complex.

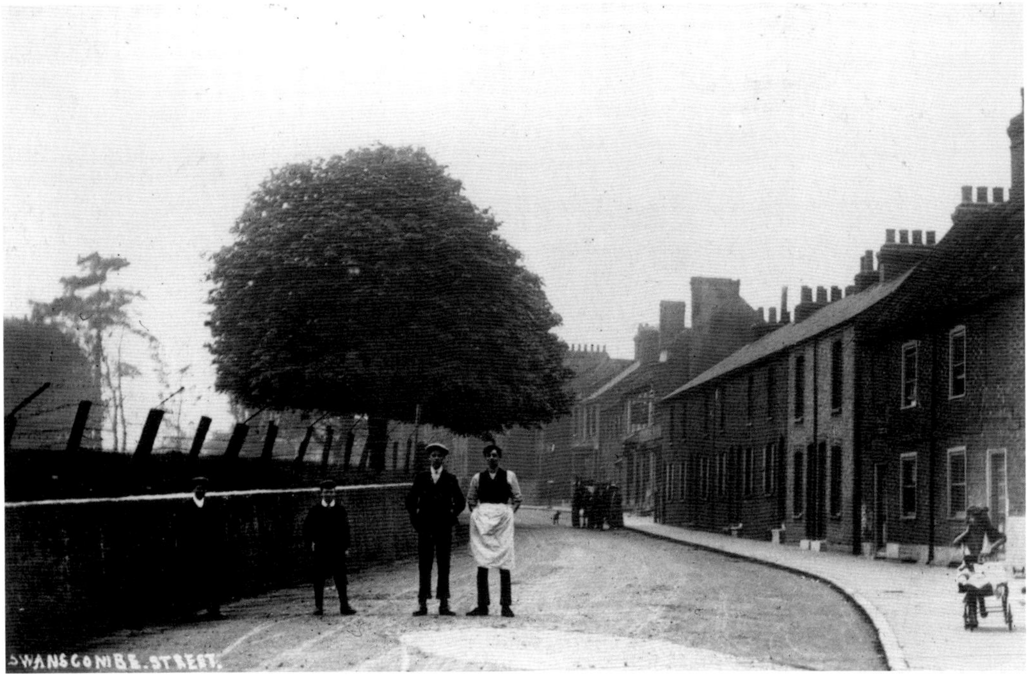

33. Swanscombe Street, looking west circa 1905. Swanscombe Street was the original village of Swanscombe before the industrial era, which created the modern High Street. Swanscombe itself was well away from the main A226 road to the north and it had the make up of a classic village: a major public house, manor house and church all in close proximity. This view shows the 'Blue Anchor' public house on the right (with sign) and a row of eighteenth- and nineteenth-century brick cottages, most of which have been demolished or greatly altered since 1905. The enclosed land on the left, above the brick wall, was an open field with two ponds separating the Manor House from the Mansion House. Part of this field was used as a Prisoner of War camp during the Second World War. The German prisoners were used to help on the farms and some married Swanscombe ladies after the war. After 1945 the camp was used to accommodate building workers who travelled to London to clear war damage. Keary Road and Munford Drive occupy the field area today. At a quick glance of this picture, one could be forgiven for thinking it was nearby Cobham or Southfleet and so shows how much of the rural pre-industrial heritage was still in existence until well into the twentieth century.

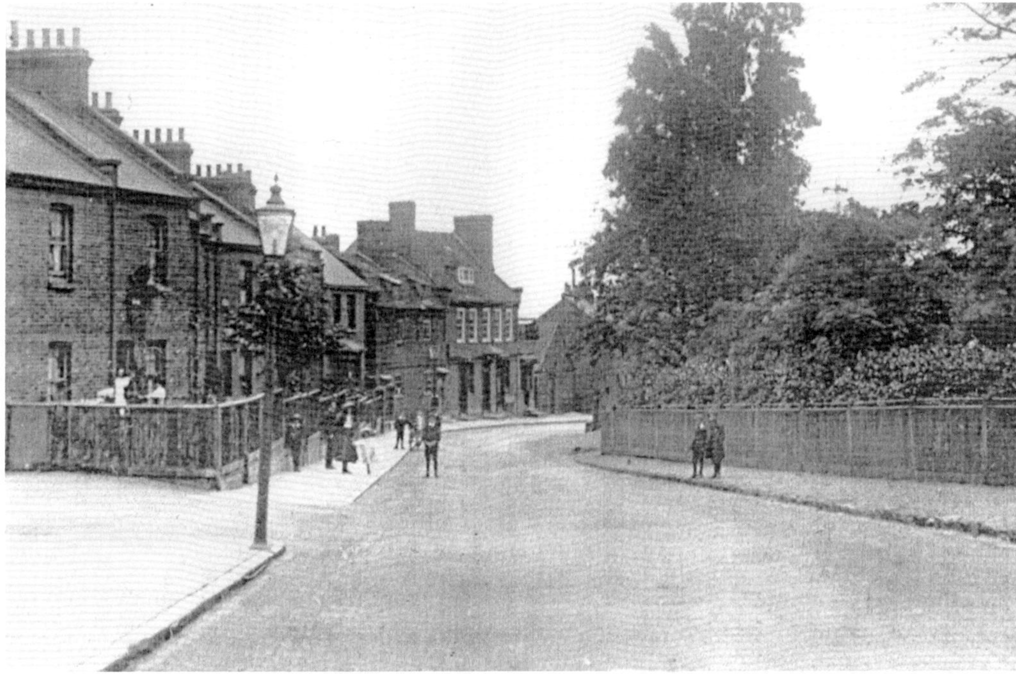

34. Swanscombe Street looking East circa 1908. On the right side is the fence of Manor Farm, which stood next to St. Peter and St. Paul's Church (see pictures 39 and 40). The farm had been owned by the cement industry since 1872 and was rented by a succession of farmers including John Westacott Gunn who ran it from about 1898 with the Gunn Family in occupation throughout the period prior to 1939.
On the left is Eglington Road with a gas lamp-post supplied by the Northfleet and Greenhithe Gas Company. The row of Victorian terraced houses sweeps down to the Blue Anchor public house and its adjacent eighteenth century cottages. Beyond the Blue Anchor is what appears to have once served as the inn's stabling facilities before the early nineteenth century houses known as Rosina Terrace begin.
Tasteless redevelopment since the 1960s has destroyed this scene apart from the now much altered Victorian cottages on the left.

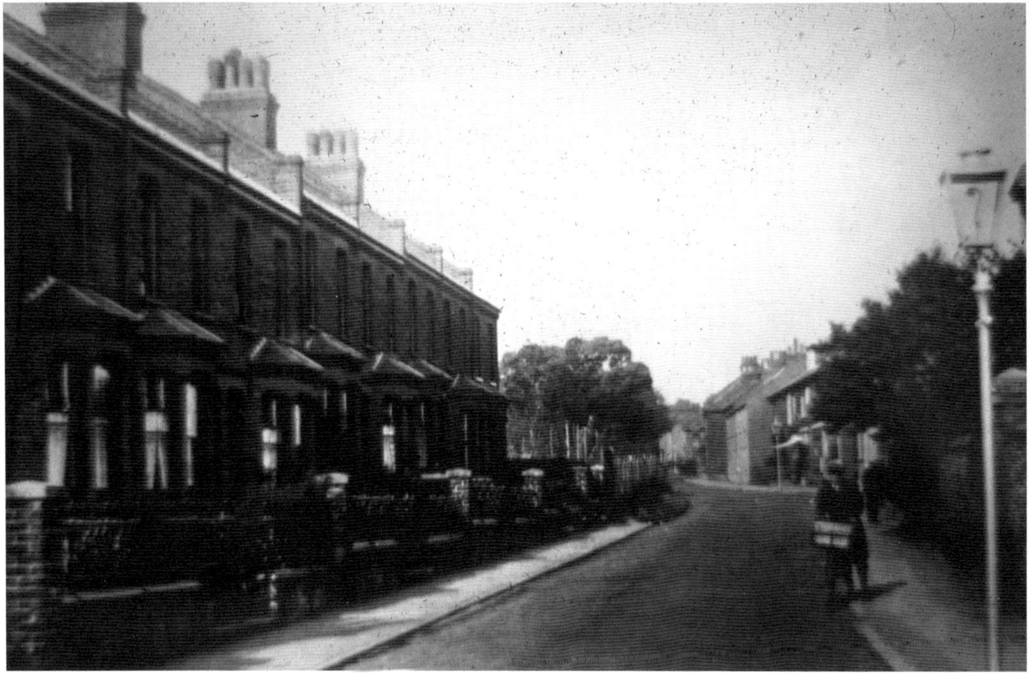

35. Swanscombe Street looking west circa 1920. The view is looking from the junction of Stanhope/Southfleet roads along Swanscombe Street. Like many streets, this has had several names. In 1881 it was Church Road, which is logical as the parish church is further along, but by 1909 it was 'High Street' and became Swanscombe Street shortly afterwards. The lamp-posts shown are gas but in 1930 a decision was taken to use electricity and by 1931 123 such lamp-posts had been converted or replaced. The houses on the left are 'White's Villas' which have an obvious connection with the White's Cement Works and were built in 1899. These replaced five farm cottages, which were sold for development in 1890. Beyond the houses is open ground occupied until the 1930s by allotment gardens, which were one of many fairly small land plots given over to providing extra food for Swanscombe's poor families. On the right can just be seen 'Combe Lodge' a large Victorian house dating from the 1850s. Its garden spread towards Stanhope Road, which was developed piecemeal from about 1902 until the 1930s when the former planned garden was covered in housing.

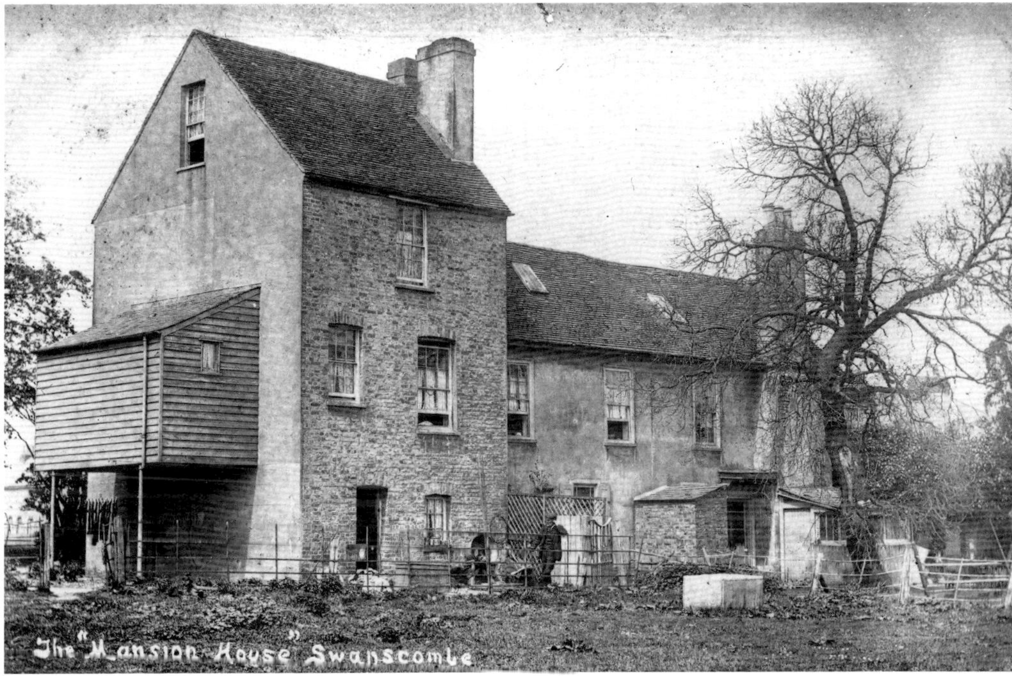

36. The Mansion House (not to be confused with the nearby Manor House) stood on the south side of Swanscombe Street almost opposite the junction with Church Road. It was believed to have been Elizabethan (1558-1603) but as this picture shows it was massively altered in the nineteenth century. During the mid- to late-nineteenth century it was occupied by various families, including the Russells, who also lived at the Manor House. John Russell was the owner of a large brewery in Gravesend and was twice mayor of that town (1876-1877 and 1898-1899). The most famous occupant was Henry Stopes and his family – especially his daughter Marie Stopes (1880-1958), the pioneer of promoting birth control in the early twentieth century. Henry Stopes rented the house for holidays in Swanscombe looking for prehistoric fossils – he was buried at Swanscombe Cemetery in 1902. The Mansion House and its estate were put up for sale in April 1890 consisting of nearly 29 acres including building land, cottages and shops dotted over Swanscombe. The Mansion House itself consisted of three floors with dining, morning, drawing rooms, six bedrooms, a library with panelled walls, two staircases, a huge kitchen, stabling and a gardener's cottage. The house was subsequently rented out, reduced in size before being demolished after 1922.

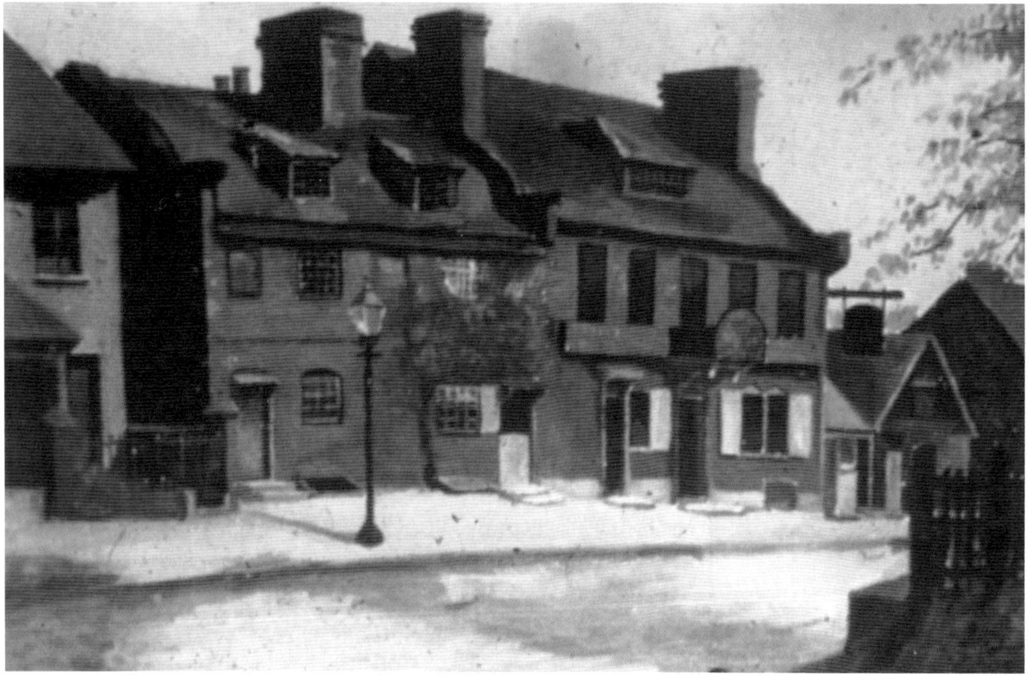

37. Blue Anchor Public House, Swanscombe Street, circa 1905. Swanscombe has had at least 25 pubs that are recorded – that excludes Greenhithe. Most public houses were 'beer houses' offering a basic service with no spirits allowed for sale. The Blue Anchor and the George & Dragon were the two premier establishments with full licenses and able to offer stabling for horses and rooms for guests. The name Blue Anchor is supposed to come from an ancient legend whereby a chain appeared from the sky one Sunday morning with an anchor at the end, which had lodged itself behind a gravestone in the churchyard. A man in sailor's costume descended the chain and in attempting to free the anchor drowned – even though he was on dry land. The chain was cut leaving him in Swanscombe. A local version of this story was that he was abandoned by the unseen vessel in the clouds, but survived to be the first landlord of the Blue Anchor. The anchor was seized by the locals, melted down and made into the hinges on the north door of St. Peter and St. Paul's church. This wonderful building, with astonishing lack of taste, was demolished and replaced with a new pub on the same site (but set further back from the road) in March 1965.

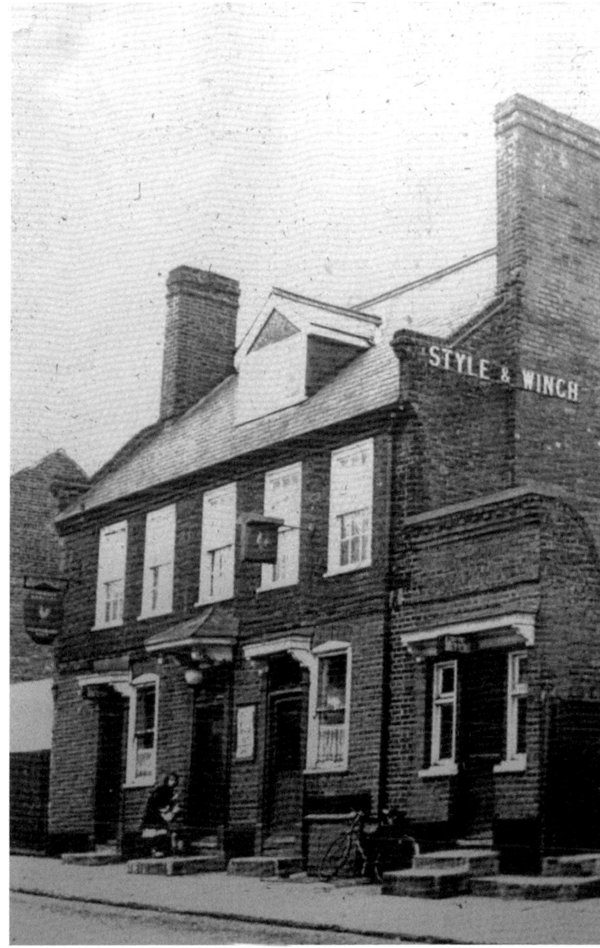

38. Blue Anchor public house, Swanscombe Street. This photograph was taken at a time of transition – Style & Winch were taken over by Courage Brewery in 1958 and both companies are still displayed. The pub was built circa 1735 in what was the original village of Swanscombe, long before the days of Galley Hill's growth in the Victorian era. Like all pubs, the Blue Anchor hosted many local organisations such as the Royal Ancient Order of Buffalos, which is a friendly society for working class people to pay small amounts of money weekly and to use in case of illness or other crises. Swanscombe United Football Club also used the premises for their headquarters. The Hazel Family were landlords from the 1890s until the early 1980s. This view shows a small entrance on the right, which led into a yard and then onto a huge 158-foot-long garden with three outside toilets. A stable was situated to the right of the above entrance (just out of the photograph) and a skittle alley was also part of the back building complex.

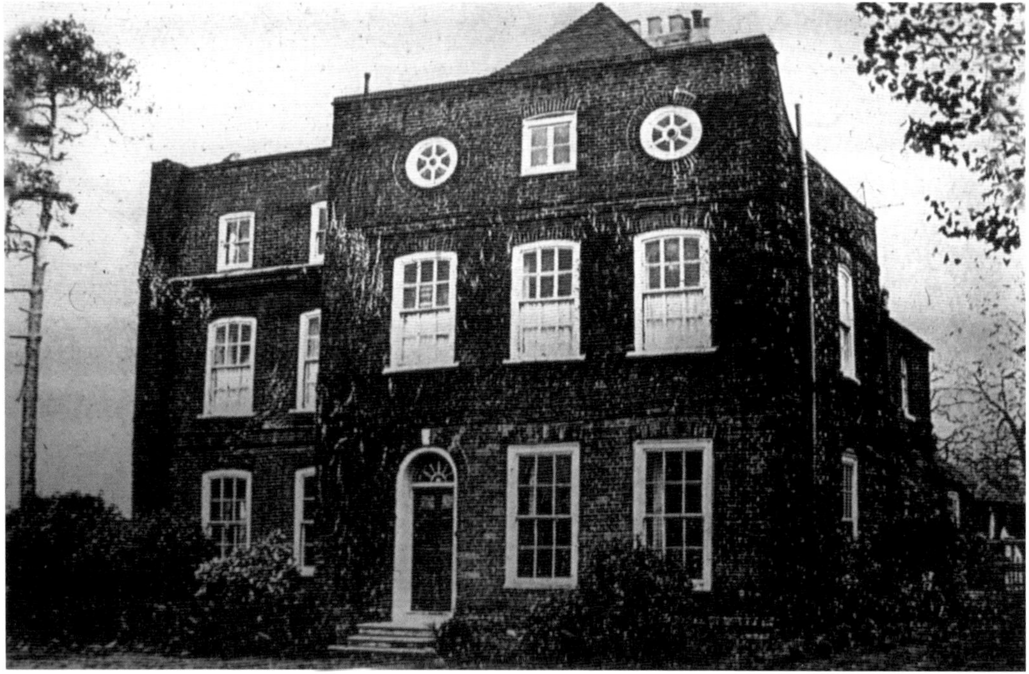

39. Manor Farmhouse, Swanscombe Street. This beautiful building probably began life as the Manor Farm rather than the Manor House, which was possibly situated at the nearby Mansion House. The Child family, who were bankers in London, owned the property from 1740 and probably created what is seen here – as the older building was encased in fashionable eighteenth century brick. In 1872 Thomas Bevan, one of the leading cement manufacturers, purchased this house, along with a vast area of Swanscombe. Over the next century more of the land was progressively turned over to chalk and clay extraction while the farm itself was tenanted out: John Coveney (1866-1880), Robert Stewart (1880-c1896). John and Jack Gunn (1890s to 1950s) and the Pallant family until the early 1960s. The Gunns were local councillors running a jam factory for their fruit (until it was burned down in the 1920s), haulage as well as farming and taking a prominent role in Swanscombe life. Jack Gunn died in 1974 aged 89. Swanscombe Urban District Council bought the house and grounds in the late 1950s and demolished Manor Farm in 1963 replacing it with modern but tasteless council offices, which were themselves demolished in 1989.

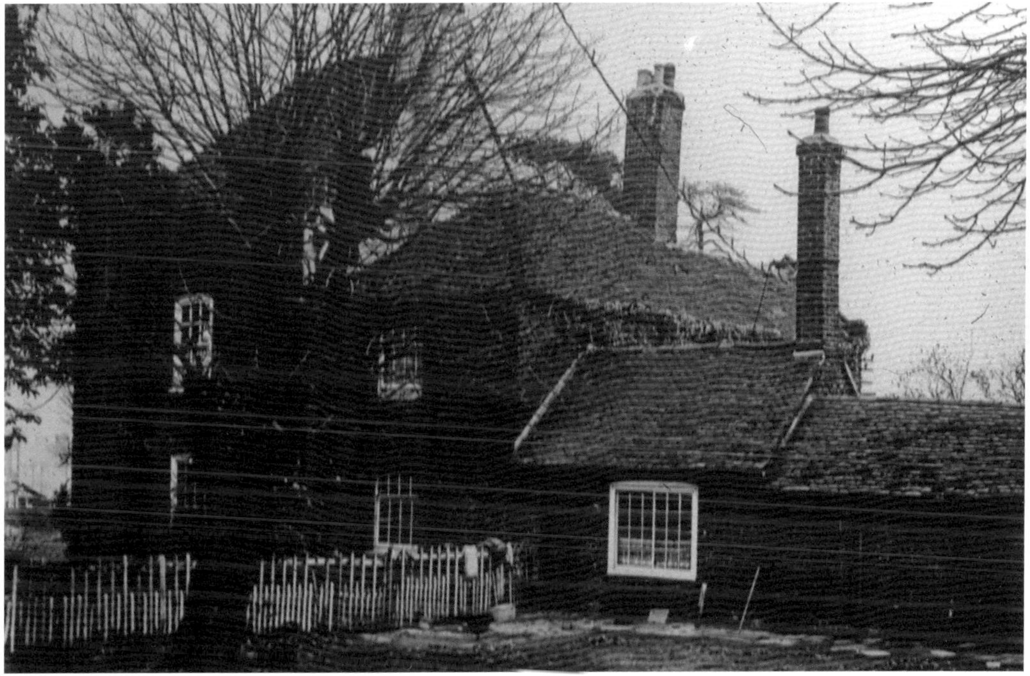

40. Rear of Manor Farmhouse, Swanscombe Street. The view shows the odd building pattern where successive rebuilding had greatly added to any surviving structure from medieval times. Manor Farm and the Mansion House nearby formed part of the Swanscombe Manor Estate until the nineteenth century and as such manorial courts were held here including, possibly, the accusation in 1652 that three Swanscombe women were witches. The Weldon family lived in the manor since the 1570s when Sir Ralph Weldon inherited the manor; both he and his wife Elizabeth have the magnificent alabaster tomb in Swanscombe Church. The Weldons had rented the manor since the 1530s prior to living in Swanscombe. The great parliamentarian leader of Kent during the Civil War (1642-1649) was Sir Anthony Weldon (1583-1648) and it was Sir Anthony who in 1613 obtained Rochester Castle and stripped it of its roof and flooring creating the ruin we see today. It was Sir Anthony who abolished Christmas in 1647 which helped cause an uprising in 1648 and it was Sir Anthony who was determined to await the royalist attack on his manor house and to die fighting – in the event he died peacefully later that year.

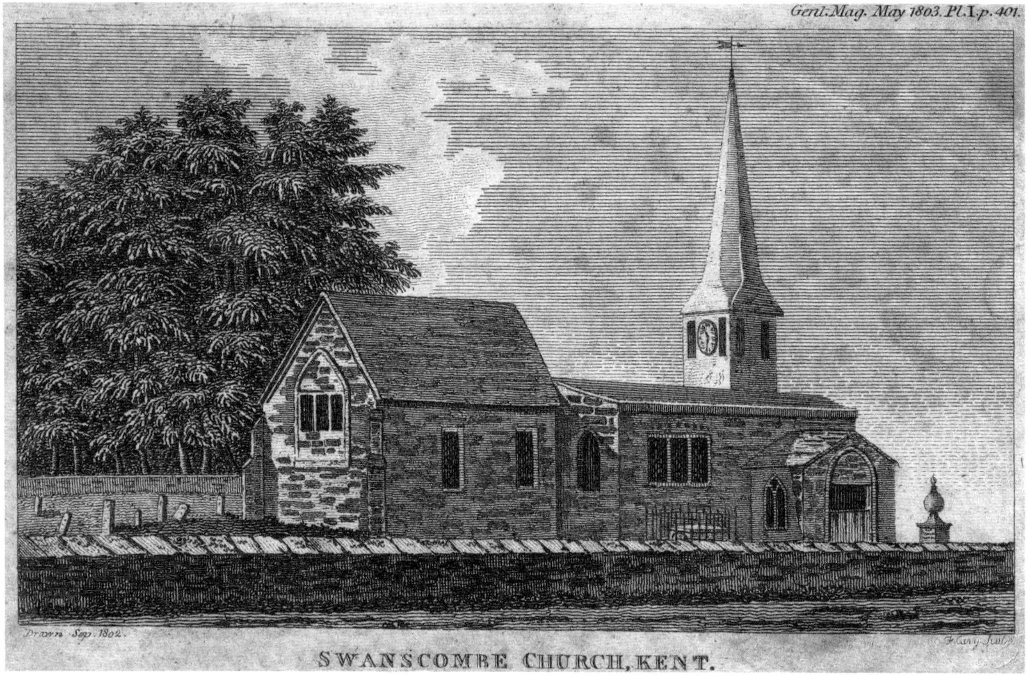

41. Swanscombe Church 1802. The above is from the Gentleman's Magazine and clearly illustrates the ancient parish church of St. Peter and St. Paul after some fairly clumsy eighteenth-century alterations.

The east window (on the left) clearly shows its medieval extent, but it had been bricked up and a mean window was inserted in its place. The porch was believed to have been much altered in the seventeenth century and did not assume its present shape until 1873. Virtually all the windows shown are not medieval but altered in a similarly crude way as the east window. This print shows the disregard for medieval features in churches before the Victorian and our own eras. Swanscombe Church was also home to a folklore event of the 'Virgin's Garlands' – a ceremony whereby adult females, who died as virgins, had garlands of flowers and coloured cloth placed on their coffin and then hung in the church as a symbol of victory over the lusts of the flesh. This ceremony survived at Swanscombe until the mid-nineteenth century – long after other parishes had abandoned it.

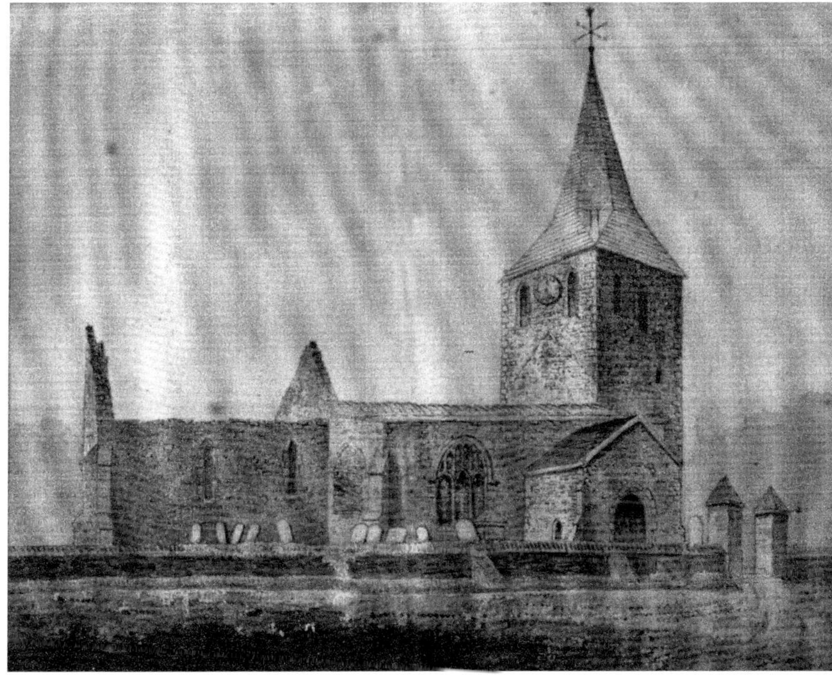

42. Swanscombe Church 1868. St. Peter and St. Paul's Church had suffered from years of neglect as was the case nationally, and it fell to the enthusiasm of the Victorians to restore thousands of parish churches. In 1868 the Reverend Thomas Candy became rector and he was a man of great energy and vision – he began a scheme to raise money for the church's restoration. Candy had already had the chancel roof removed at the time of this painting (18 July 1868) but his scheme soon ran into financial problems – especially as the White Brothers (owners of the Cement Works) were reluctant to provide any of the riches they had gained from digging huge pits in Swanscombe. The restoration was not completed until £2000 was donated by Sir Erasmus Wilson (1809-1884), the eminent skin surgeon, and the man who paid to have Cleopatra's needle shipped to London. Once Wilson's gift was known, others donated money (including the White Brothers) and the church was officially reopened on 31 October 1874.

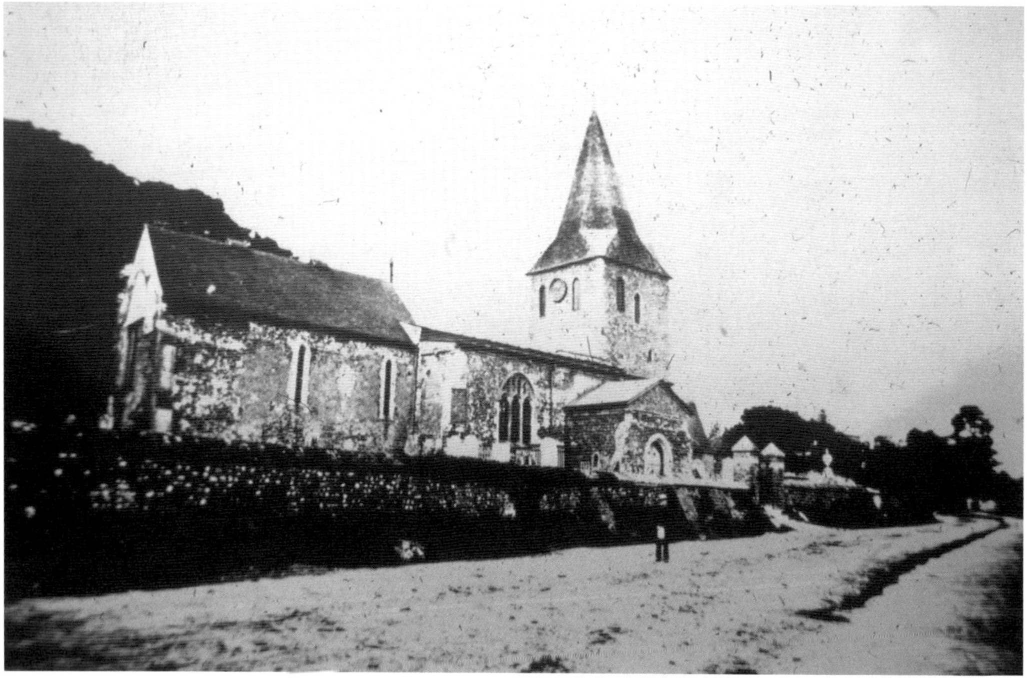

43. St. Peter and St. Paul's Church, photograph circa 1860. Compare this photograph with the previous painting. This view is of the unrestored church and shows the clock in the tower, which only faced east along Swanscombe Street rather than having a clock face on all sides of the tower. The new rector, Thomas Henry Candy (1868), received a church that had been in the care of the Reverend George Renouard for fifty years followed by the Reverend Yates, who died within months of coming to Swanscombe. Consequently little had been done and the church was old fashioned to the tastes of the Victorians. Candy's restoration dispensed with the clock, the old box pews, a gallery on the west side of the nave, and the porch was rebuilt by local freemasons.

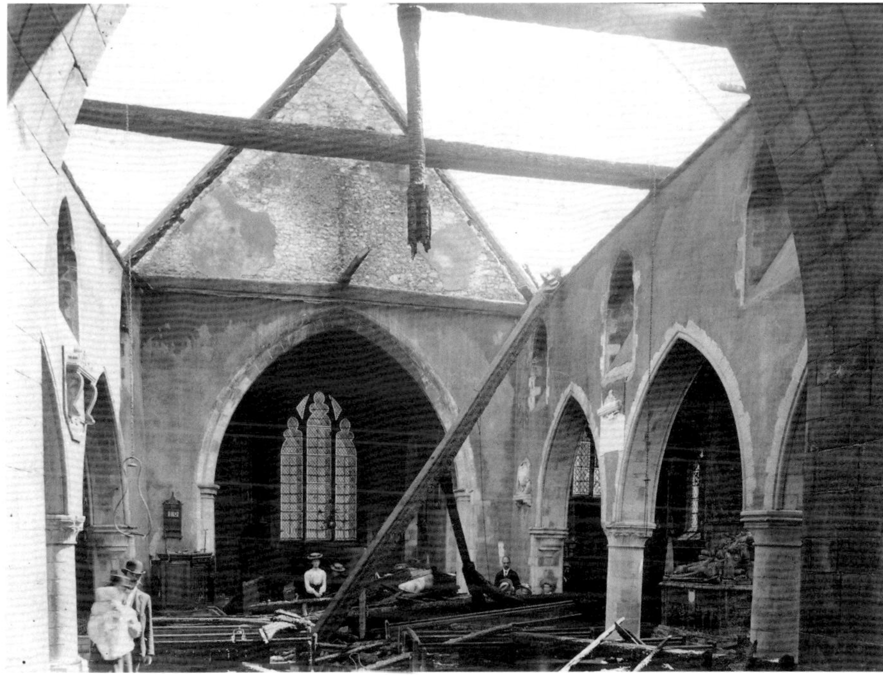

44. St. Peter and St. Paul's Church interior view after fire damage, 1902. The ancient parish church was severely damaged by a fire caused by a lightening strike on 14th August 1902. The fire destroyed the upper part of the tower melting the bells before burning the roof of the nave causing it to collapse into the church. The fledgling Swanscombe Fire Brigade with help from Northfleet desperately fought the flames but a water hydrant outside the Blue Anchor pub was accidentally damaged and the pond at the rear of the church enabled only a feeble water pressure. It was a miracle that Swanscombe Church retained most of its treasures such as the Weldon tomb, the parish registers and the ancient wooden lectern. Even the Norman font, created from a single block of chalk and broken by a falling roof beam, was subsequently repaired. The church was still used for weddings even in its ruined state but it was fully restored in June 1903 and the bells were replaced in March 1904

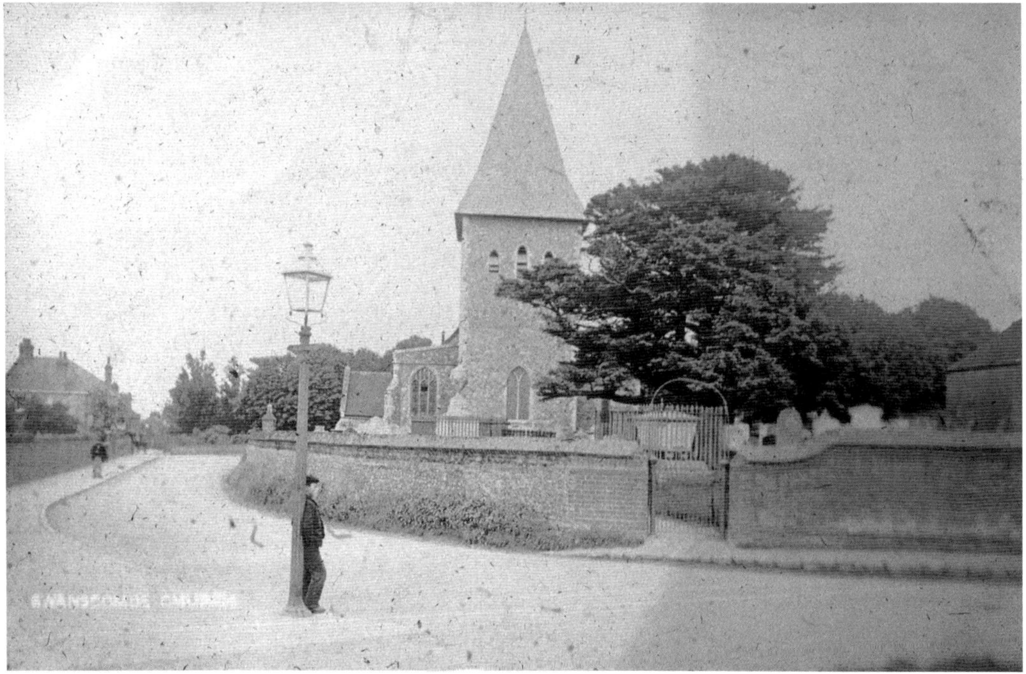

45. St. Peter and St. Paul's Church, circa 1910. The photograph shows the parish church after its restoration in 1903-1904 having recovered from the disastrous fire of 1902. The rural nature of Swanscombe can be gleaned by noting the oast house and barn on the right and the trees surrounding the Manor House in the background. The growing urban nature of Swanscombe can be seen by the gas lamp-posts, the made-up pavement and the cemetery wall on the left.

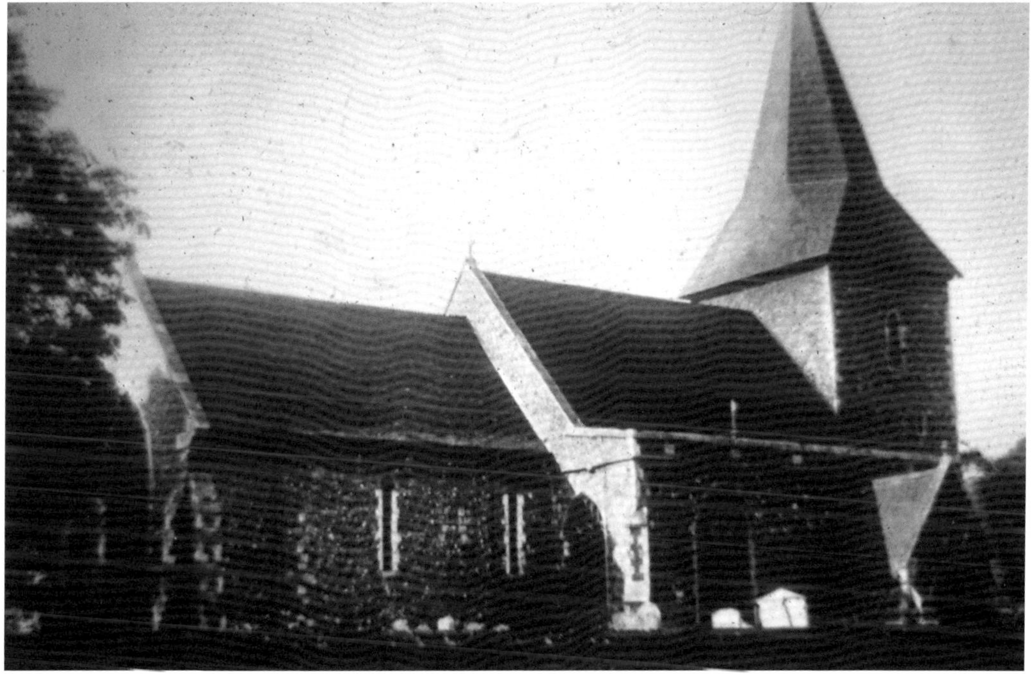

46. St. Peter and St. Paul's church circa 1930. Here is the result of the Reverend T.H. Candy's effort in restoring the church, completed in 1874, and then having to be re-restored after the fire of 1902. The nave roof had been raised in height and a peel of eight new bells replaced the six dating from 1751 that had melted in the fire of 1902. The new bells were dedicated by the Venerable Dr. Cheetham, Archdeacon of Rochester, on 5th March 1904, but 92 years of ringing Swanscombe's great events meant a huge restoration of the bells, their fittings and the tower in 1994-1995. The bells have been ringing regularly again since December 1996. In 1995 the churchyard became the fourth home since 1958 of the Invicta monument, which records the legend of William of Normandy (William the Conqueror) being forced by a Kentish army at Swanscombe to retain Kent's ancient rights in 1066. The monument began life in 1958 along the A2 (Watling Street - site of the legend). It was then moved to Swanscombe Urban District Council's offices in 1965 (after the A2 was widened), and then into a store after the council offices were demolished in 1989. Finally the stone was put into the churchyard for all to see.

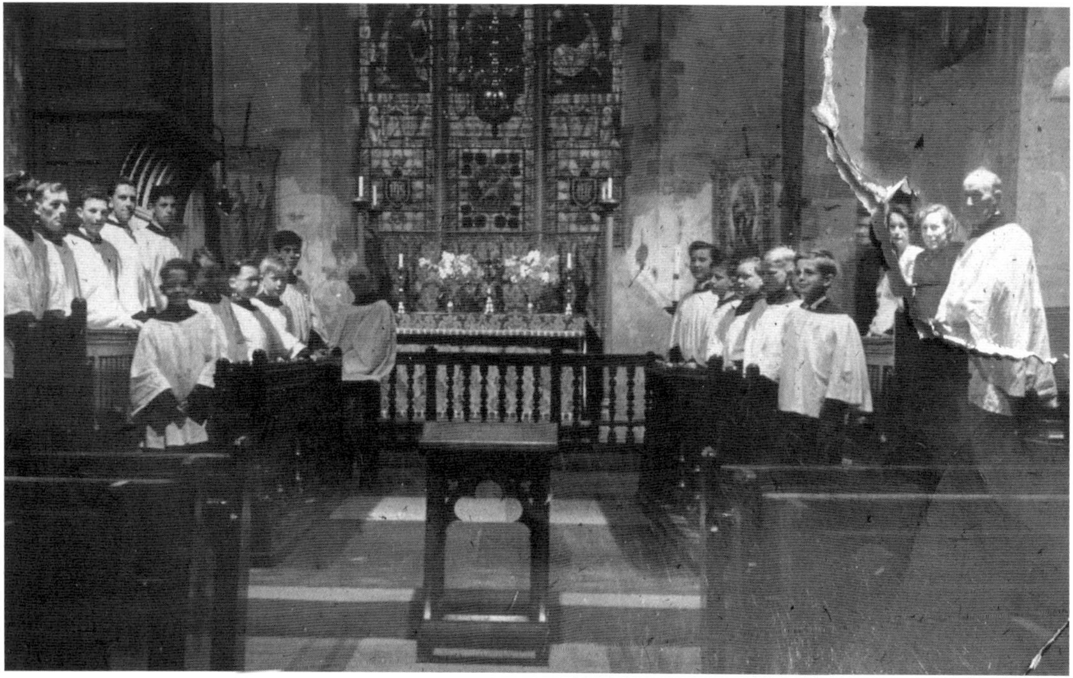

47. Choir, St. Peter and St. Paul's church. The view dates from the 1950s. The alter rails and alter are in their traditional position at the east of the church chancel although they now occupy a central site in the chancel following changes in 1971. The alter is wooden and dates from 1902 but it has a medieval stone alter top inserted into it. The organ on the left was installed by the Reverend Candy in the 1870s and built by Henry Fincham of London – the organ has since been replaced by an electronic version. The scene is illuminated with gas lights (on right-hand side), and the pews were those installed in the restoration of 1873 but again replaced after the fire of 1902. This view remained largely unchanged until internal alteration since the 1960s and 1970s.

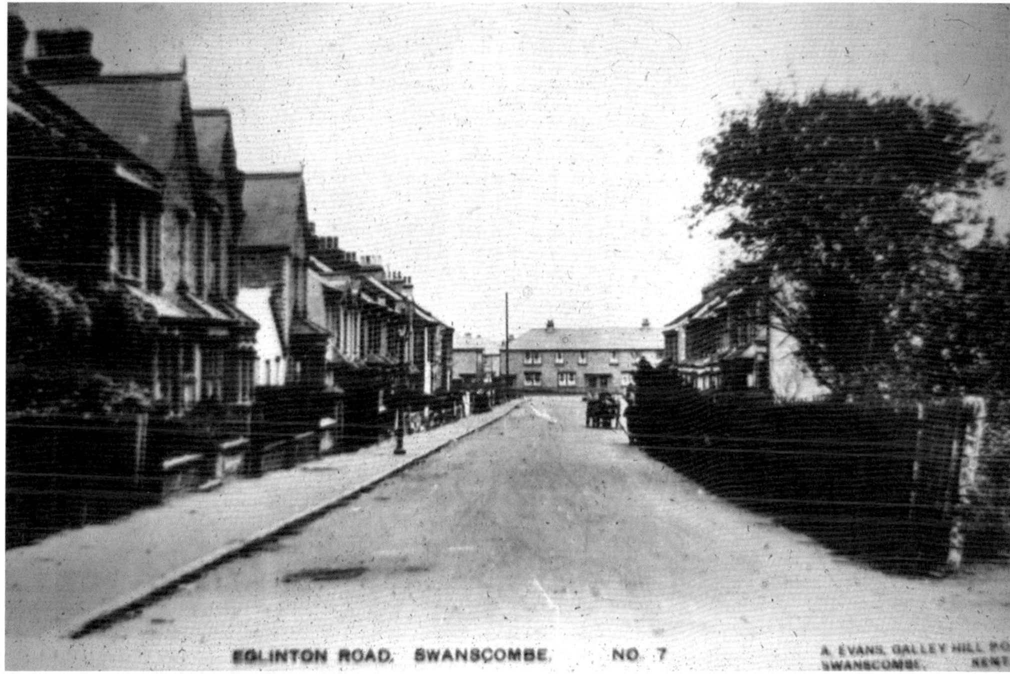

48. Eglington Road, Swanscombe circa 1930. This road was one of a clutch of new developments coming off the original road of Swanscombe Street. The first eleven plots for building were those occupied by the houses on the left and were sold in 1885. By 1890 more empty plots were again up for sale. On the right can be seen the last few trees of a once considerable orchard before the site was covered with houses by the 1930s. In the distance can be seen Ames Road, a development largely undertaken by Swanscombe Urban District Council after 1926 in an attempt to relieve overcrowding, provide decent housing for working people and to expand the population of the town. Eglington Road was also the site of Barker's shop – famed for its high quality ice cream, which was sold from the shop and via a tricycle with a special modified front so that the ice cream could be transported around Swanscombe. In 1973 Miss Ivy Barker saw off a youth brandishing a knife in the shop and demanding money. Barker's shop did eventually close down and has not traded since the 1980s.

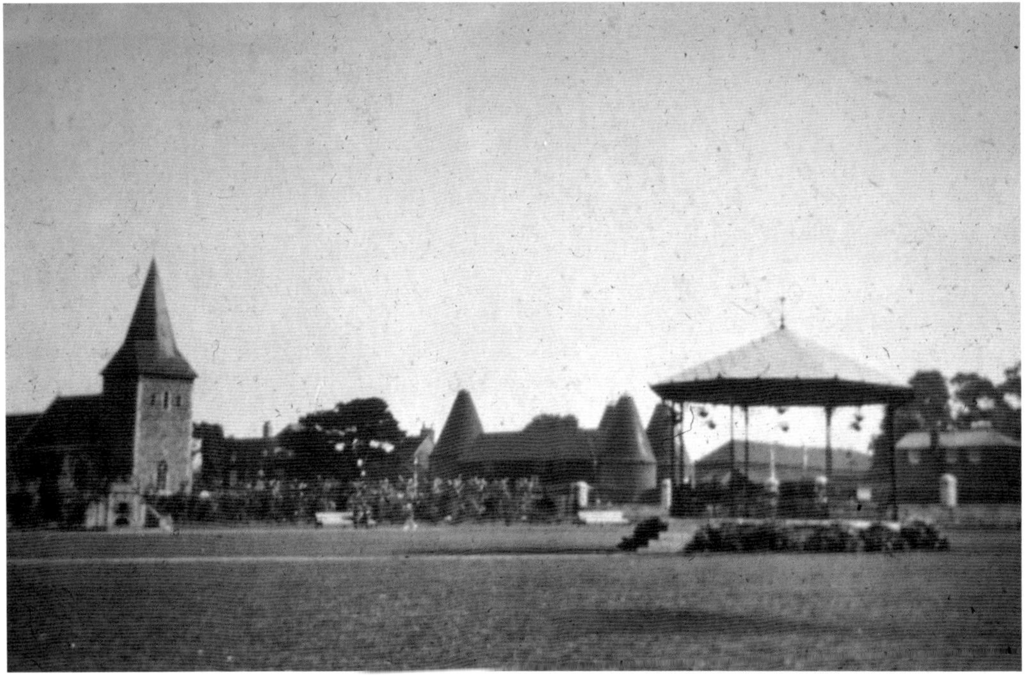

49. Swanscombe Recreation Ground 1932. The opening of the new Recreation Ground on 30 April 1932 was one of Swanscombe's great days of civic history. Swanscombe Urban District Council, using locally produced materials and local unemployed men to create this magnificent new facility, had relieved the appalling high rate of unemployment. The opening day was a Saturday with warm sunshine and was attended by crowds of local people in addition to civic dignitaries from Swanscombe, Northfleet, Gravesend and Stone. The ground was officially opened by Councillor Alexander Entwhistle, the chairman of the council for 1930-1931 amid a huge sense of local pride and achievement. This view shows the new bandstand, the hop kilns and oast houses in the background (now used as an old people's welfare and social centre) and the boundary between the park and the cemetery. In an age of simple pleasures 'Rose Sunday' attracted crowds to the park and cemetery to see the exceptional displays of Swanscombe roses.

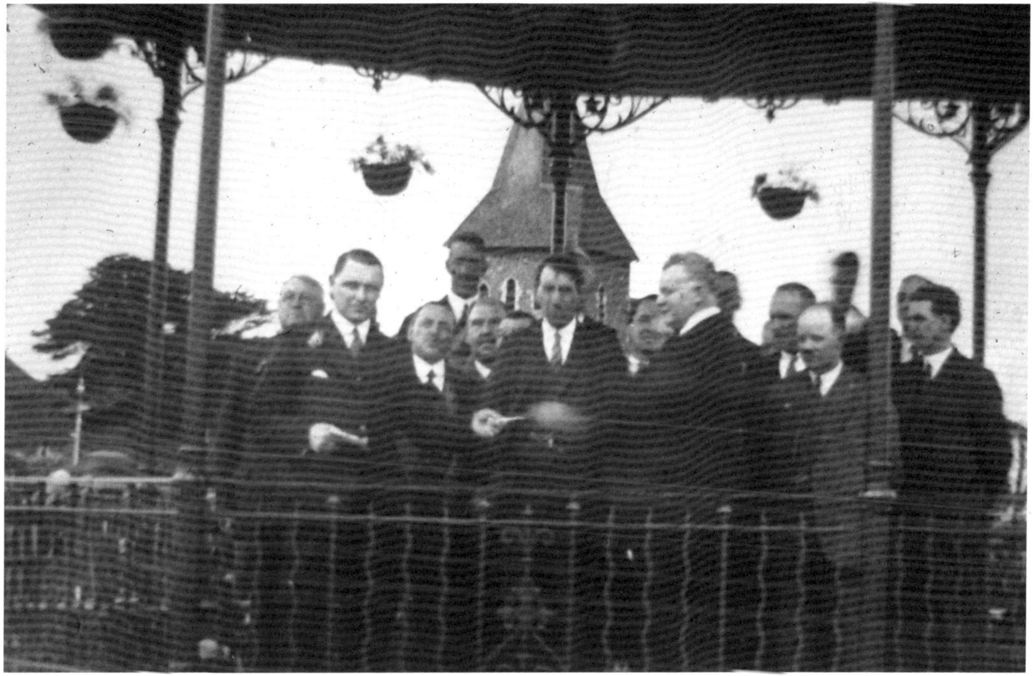

50. Swanscombe Councillors, 1932. The proud civic day of the official opening of Swanscombe's Recreation Ground on 30th April 1932 is shown here with the local councillors and officials gathered on the bandstand. The three councillors at the front are: (left) William Everard of Everards, the shipping company in Greenhithe, who was chairman of the Unemployment Grants Scheme Committee. In the centre is Thomas Broad, chairman of Swanscombe Urban District Council 1932-33 and chairman of the Works Committee. On the right is Alexander Entwhistle, chairman of the Urban District Council 1930-1932 who is accepting the silver key to officially open the Recreation Ground. Other councillors present on this occasion were John Gunn (of Manor Farm), Walter Ames (see picture 22), William Knight, Thomas Wedgewood Ostle, Thomas Tutt, Arthur Allen, Thomas Bodle, Albert Frost, Arthur Lane, Thomas Coveney, Stanley Fright, Peter Fletcher and R.W. Butcher.

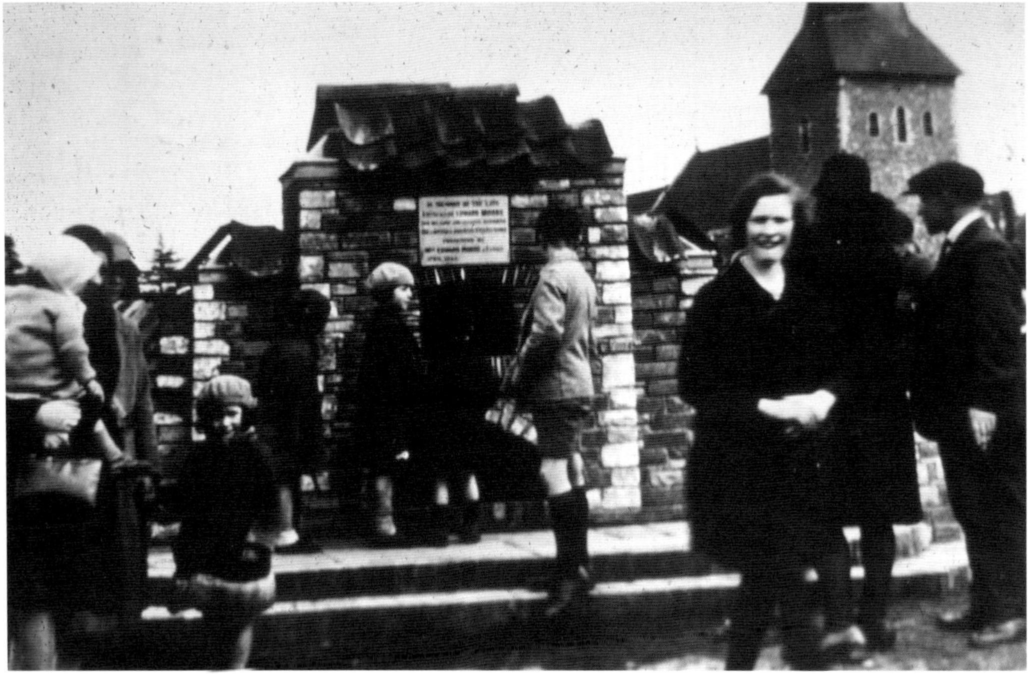

51. Memorial Fountain, Recreation Ground, Swanscombe, 1932. The fountain is part of the facilities of the Recreation Ground, dedicated to the memory of Councillor Edward Moore, who died in 1932. Moore was part of a political dynasty whose financial security was originally in the Moore Brothers Mineral Water Company of 59 Milton Road, Swanscombe. Edward Moore lived in Dartford but represented Galley Hill Ward on Swanscombe Urban District Council. Moore was a very keen councillor in the creation of a 'Better and Brighter Swanscombe' campaign during the 1920s and 1930s, of which the Recreation Ground formed part. Another member of the Moore Family was George Moore, who was chairman of Swanscombe's council in 1936-1937. The fountain provided water for humans at the top and at the bottom was another watering area for dogs. Today the fountain exists but no longer provides water.

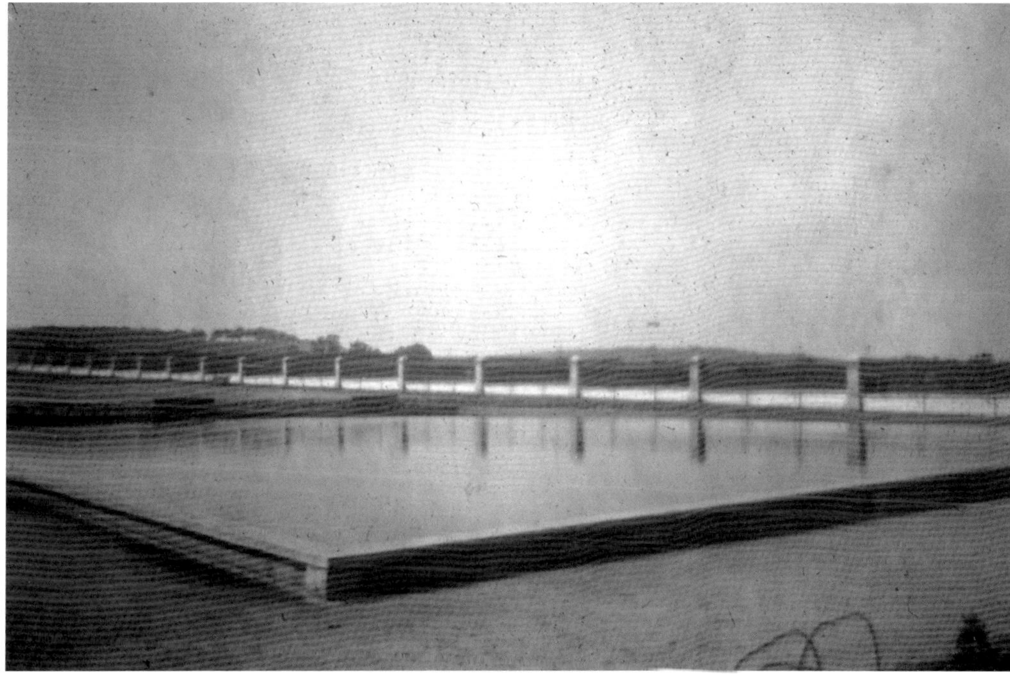

52. Boating Pond, Recreation Ground, Swanscombe, 1932. A major feature of Swanscombe's new Recreation Ground was the boating pond which, despite many local children falling in, was visited by people from miles around the area. The pond was greatly used by model boat enthusiasts and in the 1930s saw many 'pop-pop' boats on it. These were powered by a candle, which heated a tiny boiler in the vessel, thus creating steam and this caused the popping noise as the boats went across the water. Sailing boats, barges, clockwork boats were all seen on the pond. Elderly residents' model sailing boats that floated off had to be rescued by the local youth who waded into the pond with rolled-up trousers to retrieve the vessels. During the Second World War, by which time the pond was already leaking, this facility was used for roller-skating and cycles – having been drained of water first! The railings behind mark where Park Road was about to be built and in the background can be seen Swanscombe Woods on its hilly position – a place beloved by Swanscombe folk for picnics.

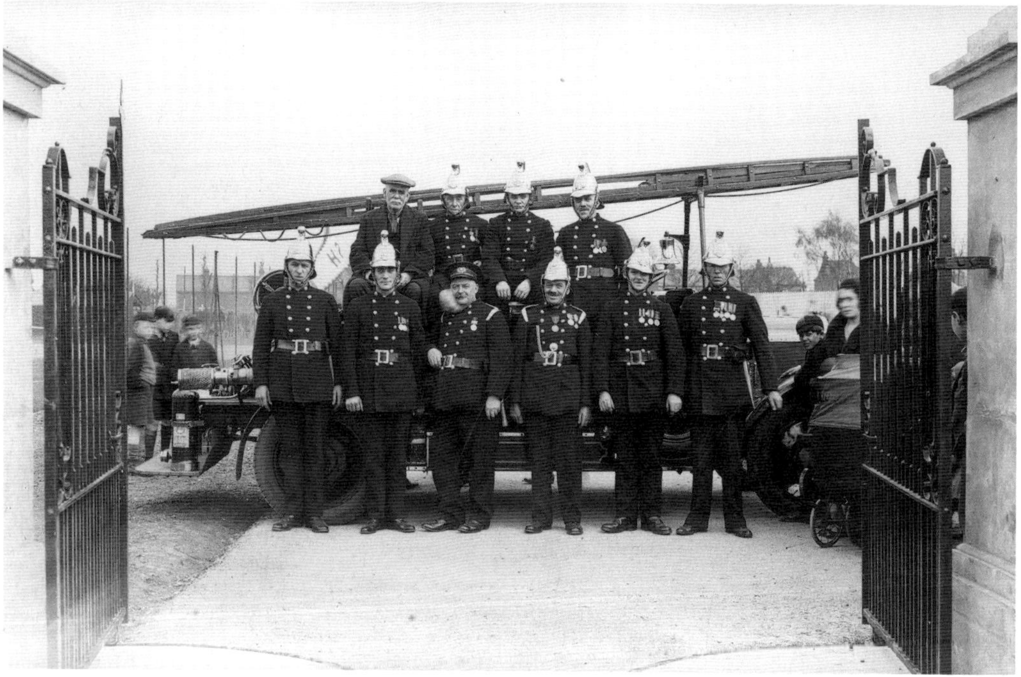

53. Swanscombe fire engine, Recreation Ground, 1932. The vehicle shown is the new purpose-built Dennis fire engine, which replaced the previous Garfield converted motorised lorry as the urban district's main fire fighting appliance in 1929. The new engine, a source of immense civic pride, stands in the entrance of another huge piece of Swanscombe's achievements, namely the Recreation Ground (as described in the previous pictures). All these and many more similar civic achievements were part of the 'Better and Brighter Swanscombe' campaign, which was such a driving force in the town after it became an independent urban district council in 1926. Captain Albert Ernest Kent is fourth from left in the front row. Kent retired from fire fighting in 1929 after a stroke, but remained as chief for ceremonial occasions after this. Next to Captain Kent can be seen Burt Ellen, with a huge goitre on the side of his face.

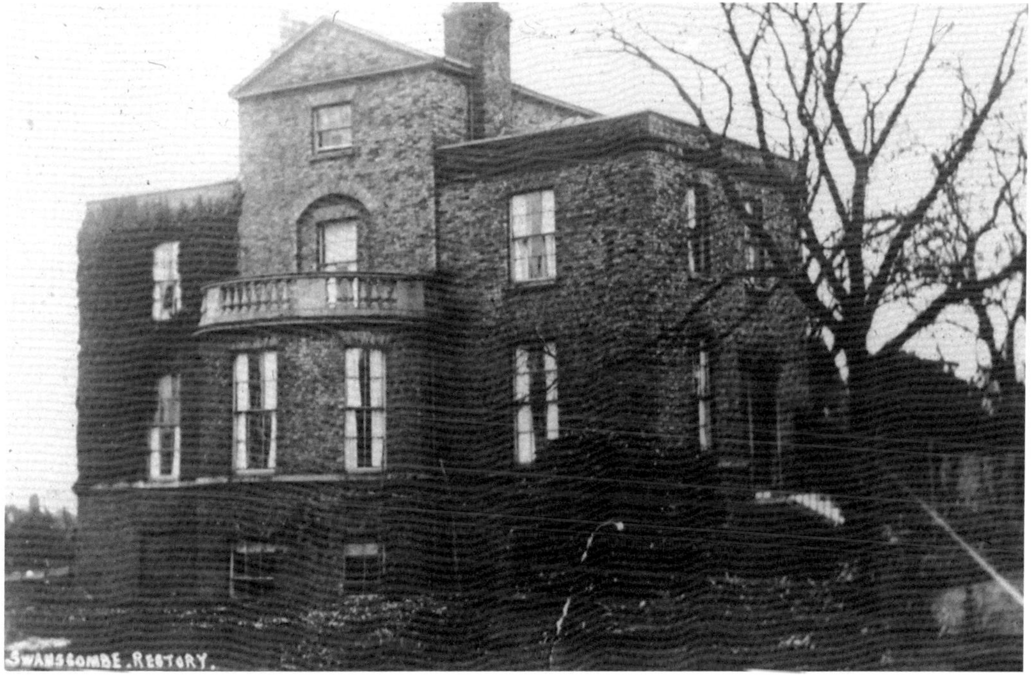

54. Swanscombe Rectory. This wonderful building was another victim of a trend within the Church of England to sell off assets and replace them with smaller modern houses and this happened at Swanscombe in the early 1960s. This building was constructed by Reverend George Cecil Renouard (Rector 1818-1867), who ran a private school from its extensive rooms. One of the pupils was Sir Erasmus Wilson (1809-1884), who became a great surgeon, brought Cleopatra's needle to London and gave much money for the church's restoration in 1873. Renouard's rectory replaced an earlier structure, which doubled as a rectory and farm – the latter bringing in an income for the rector. A successor to Renouard as rector was Reverend Thomas Candy (rector 1868-1888) who established an early public library in a room in this building from 1887. The present rectory and church centre stand on the site of this building as well as some housing development.

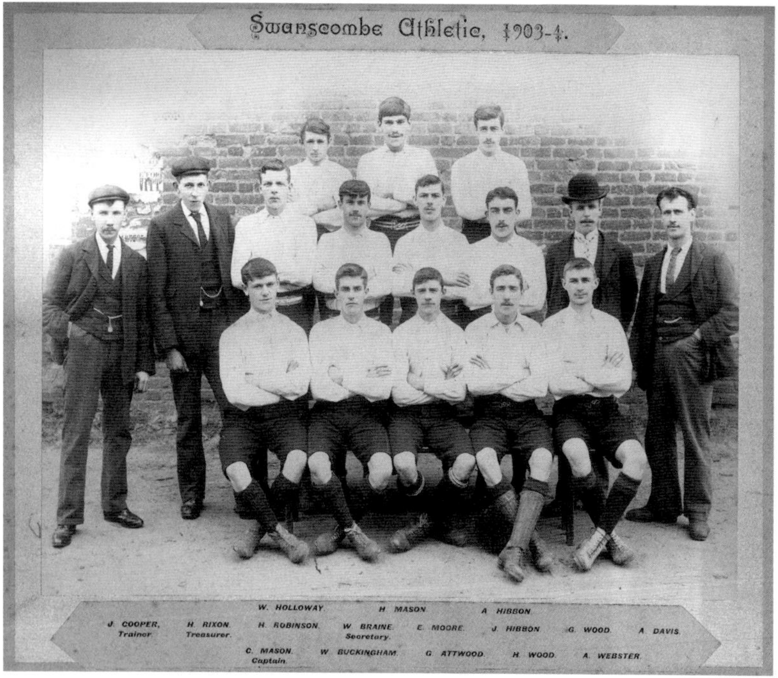

55. Swanscombe Athletic Football Club, 1903-1904. Working hours were still very long compared to today, some 54 hours a week for a cement worker in 1903 – but there was a gradual increase in leisure time. Consequently various organisations grew up such as sports clubs, political parties, cultural organisations and horticultural/livestock societies. The famous Swanscombe United Football Club with their red and black strip was the senior team, but Swanscombe Invicta was a rival. The team shown here was a break away from Invicta who, in 1903, became Swanscombe Athletic and probably shared the ground on the Rectory Field with the parent club. Swanscombe Athletic described itself as 'medium strength team, average age 19, with private ground and dressing room' in 1904, and could attract large crowds to matches: 1,000 watched a Swanscombe Invicta match in April 1904. Mr. Braine, the secretary on the picture, lived in Railway Street, Northfleet. Rivals Swanscombe United had their home pitch on land to the west of the cemetery (see picture 60) and after 1932 the whole playing area was upgraded as part of the Recreation Ground. Swanscombe Athletic, unlike rivals United, does not exist today.

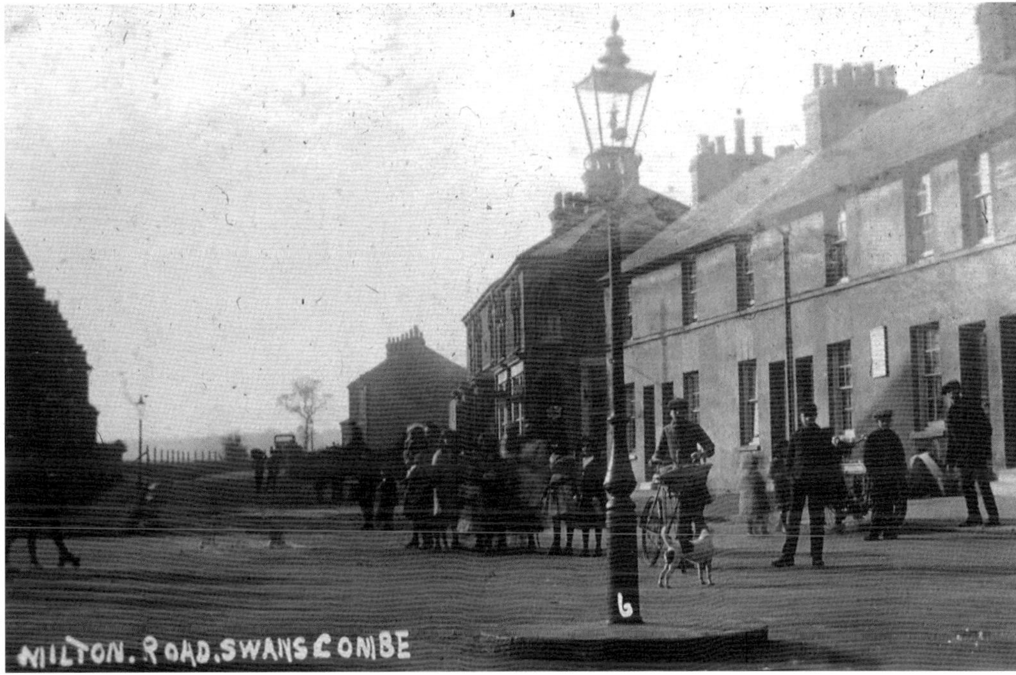

56. Milton Road, Swanscombe, circa 1920. The lamp-post supplied by Northfleet & Greenhithe Gas Works is strategically placed at the junction of the High Street, Church Road and Milton Road. Discussions were held in 1854 for the provision of streetlights in Swanscombe and they were in operation by the late nineteenth century. The row of cottages on the right was demolished in about 1961 to make way for the rash of 1960s shops. Further along on the right are the two shops of Mr. Mercer (owner of the cinema and local councillor) and Harry Town (fruiter and dairy) – the latter had an early public telephone. On the left is the corner of the Primitive Methodist Church with a dozen cottages beyond which were open fields looking across towards Milton Street. The open ground was developed by Swanscombe Urban District Council in its campaign to improve housing within the town and the roads of Ames, Gasson, Stanley and Sweyne all now cover this area. Ames, Gasson and Stanley are all named after Swanscombe councillors and the roads were in existence by 1929.

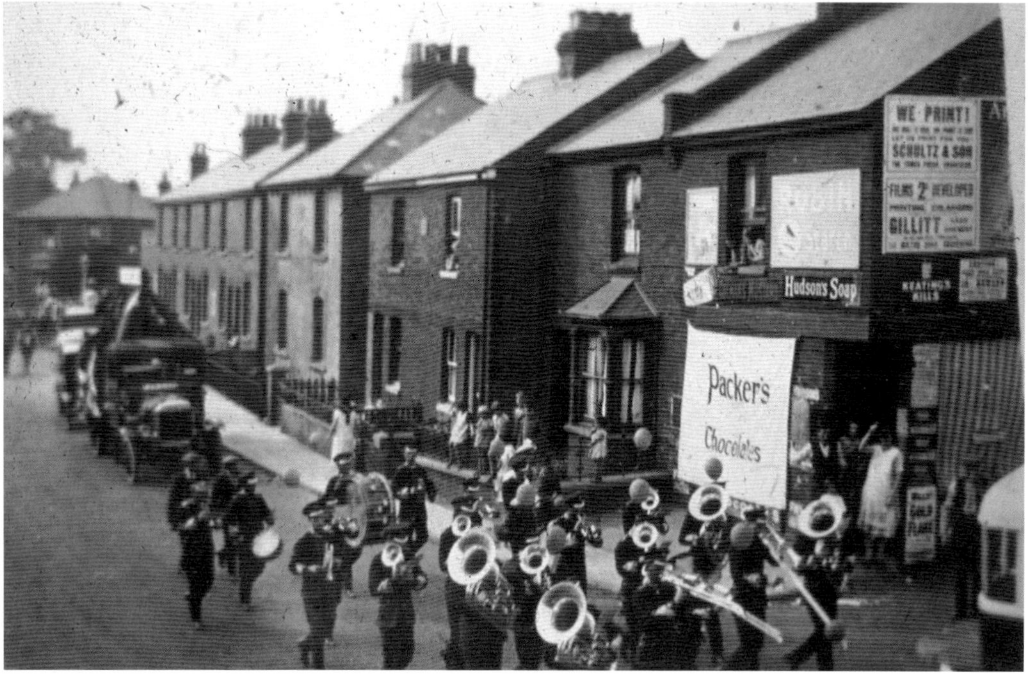

57. Brotherhood Band, Milton Road, Swanscombe, circa 1936. Part of the Gravesend and North Kent Hospital Carnival – a fund raising annual event which snaked its route via Swanscombe and Greenhithe on to Northfleet and Gravesend. The shop in the picture is that of F.V. Jones, a general shop selling groceries and greengroceries as well. One of Swanscombe's three police constables (P.C William Sage) lived in the fifth house after the shop. At the very end of the terrace was a single story building, which had been a private school known as the 'Kirteen' Private School, which was in operation by 1887 but had closed by 1906. The band was one of many in Swanscombe – this one from one of the many chapels in the town.

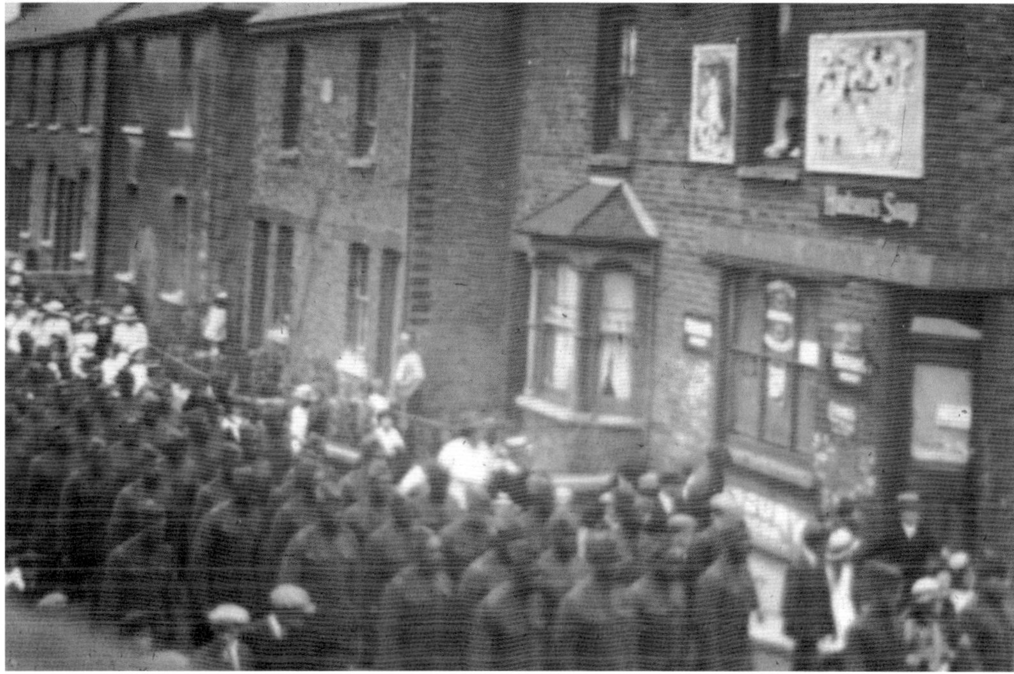

58. Black Soldiers, Milton Road, 1918. The same view as picture 57 showing Negro American soldiers marching to work at the Swanscombe Cement Factory. Swanscombe Cement Works lost vast numbers of its workforce to the army and navy – these were replaced by women and by black American troops who loaded cement required by the American forces for the war effort. Until this time non-white faces were almost unknown and after 1918 the black Americans left. During the 1920s and 1930s an occasional Indian visited Swanscombe selling silks and other goods from a suitcase. It has only been since the 1970s that larger numbers of ethnic minorities have lived in Swanscombe.

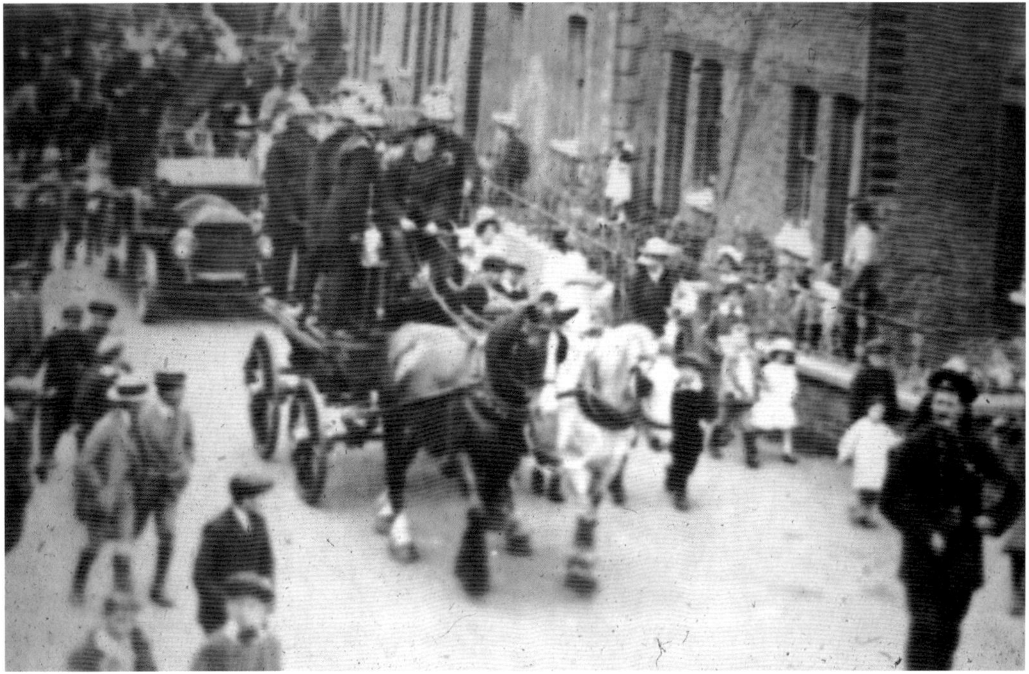

59. Fire Brigade in carnival, Milton Road, Swanscombe circa 1929. The photograph was taken at almost the same point as the previous two photographs and is part of the Gravesend and North Kent Hospital Carnival – a time of great community involvement in raising money essential for the hospital's maintenance. Swanscombe sent its patients to the hospital at Gravesend, rather than Dartford. The first fire engine was the horse-drawn manual pump purchased around 1903. Behind it appears to be the Garfield converted vehicle used by the fire brigade in the 1920s until replaced in 1930. The horse-drawn engine was only used on occasions such as this and its replacement was a Fiat vehicle, which appears to have retained the hand pump equipment from the horse-drawn engine. The fiat was sold to Hoo St. Werburgh Parish Council as their fire engine in 1930 for £10.

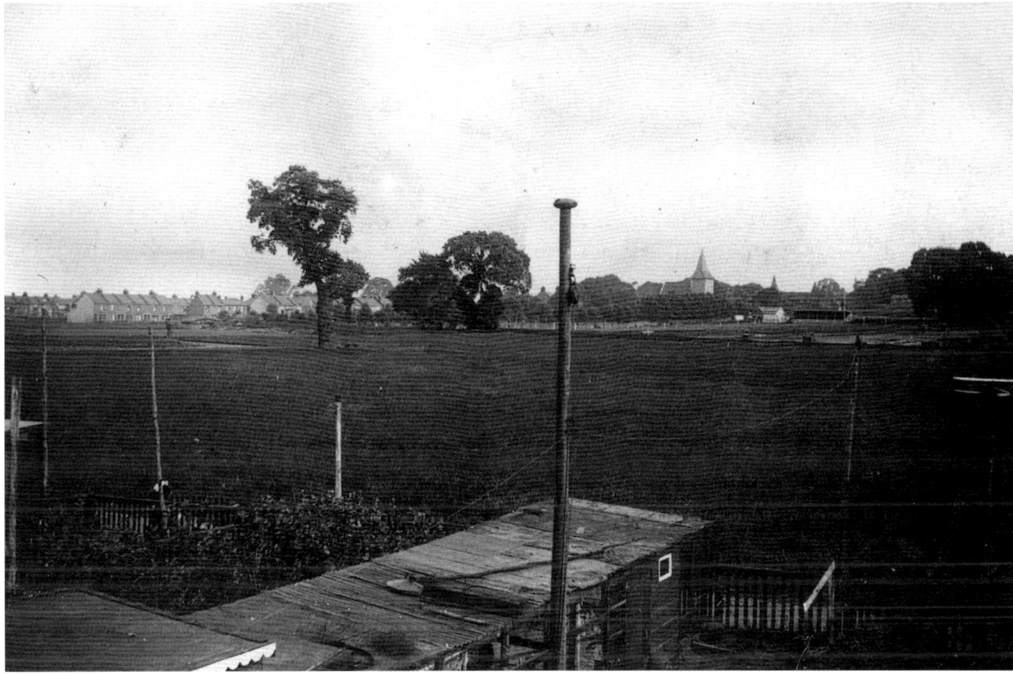

60. View from the rear of Milton Road. This picture looks south towards St. Peter and St. Paul's Church. The ramshackled sheds and outbuildings in the foreground are from houses in Milton Road. The field behind was still under cultivation and shows the site of Lewis, Ames, Moore, Broad and Gunn roads and so predates the first of the above streets (Ames Road), which had been completed by 1929. Another missing feature is the Swanscombe Recreation Ground, the site of which appears to be the ground of Swanscombe United Football Club. This gives an excellent impression of how what is now one large area of housing, originally grew piecemeal in the interwar years, covering the rural nature of Swanscombe.

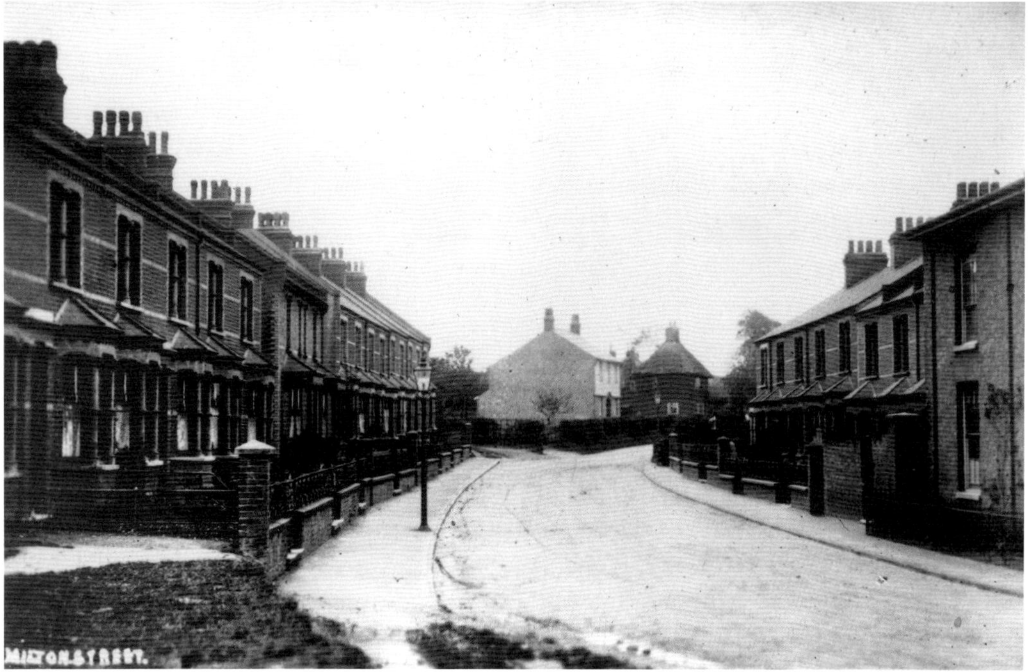

61. Milton Street, Swanscombe circa 1912. A view looking south-west. On the right stand the Victorian houses known as 'Pustwell Villas' (dated 1898) with Victorian terraced houses on both sides of the road dating from the 1890s and early 1900s. The houses on the right were all destroyed on 27th February 1945 (V2 rocket), killing eight people and injuring 48 – only one house survived. The street is still mud but gas lamp-posts show the increasing urbanisation of the area. The white house in the centre of this picture is the Swanscombe Consolidated Almshouse Charity which has its origins in numerous sixteenth- to nineteenth-century parish bequests for the poor which were amalgamated to create this dwelling for four poor people. The house was opened in 1911 and was subsequently refurbished in 1980. The final house is a thatched Kentish weatherboard house of the late seventeenth or eighteenth century and consists of two dwellings. Buildings such as these were very common in most local villages but they were seen as 'slums' and lacking in modern amenities – especially after the 1920s, when they were mercilessly demolished by local authorities. The last of these types of cottages in Swanscombe were demolished in November 1971.

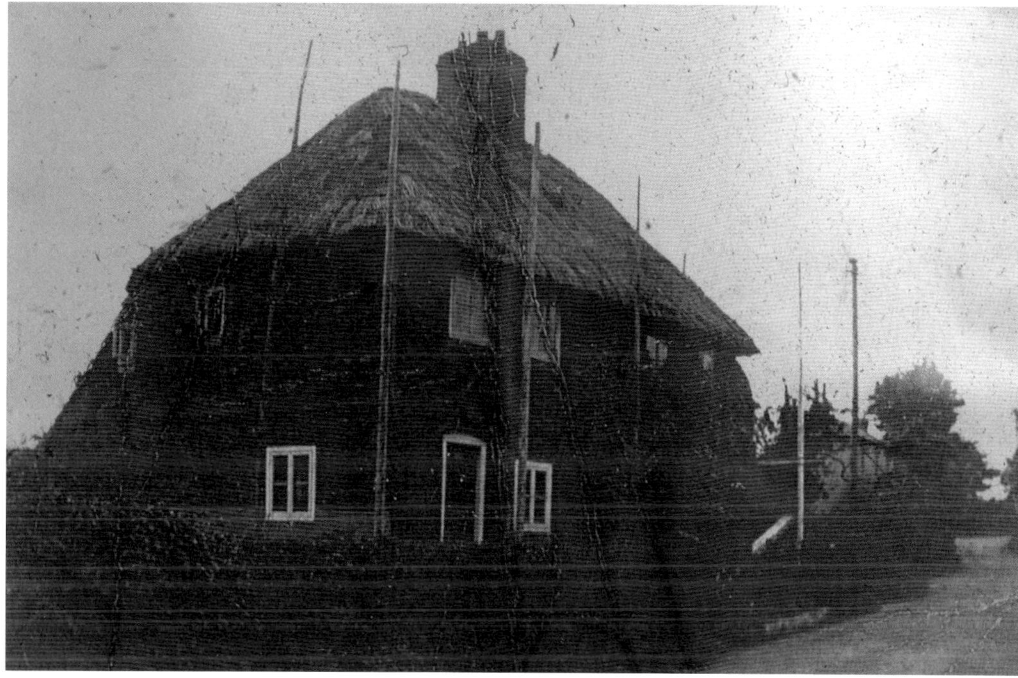

62. Thatch Cottage, Milton Street. A closer look at the two Kentish weatherboard cottages, seen in the previous picture. In the background can be seen Milton Street snaking its way towards Manor Road and Alkerden Lane. The Woodman public house can just be seen behind, which closed 1913-1914. As mentioned the last of these types of cottages survived until 1971 when, with the usual complete absence of imagination by the planners, they were demolished. The open country seen in the background of this picture is now covered with housing such as Alamein Road, built in the later 1940s, and Child's Crescent, Wallace Gardens and Wright Close, built in the 1950s. Behind the cottages are apple orchards with a notice warning against trespassing as 'gin traps' await thieves.

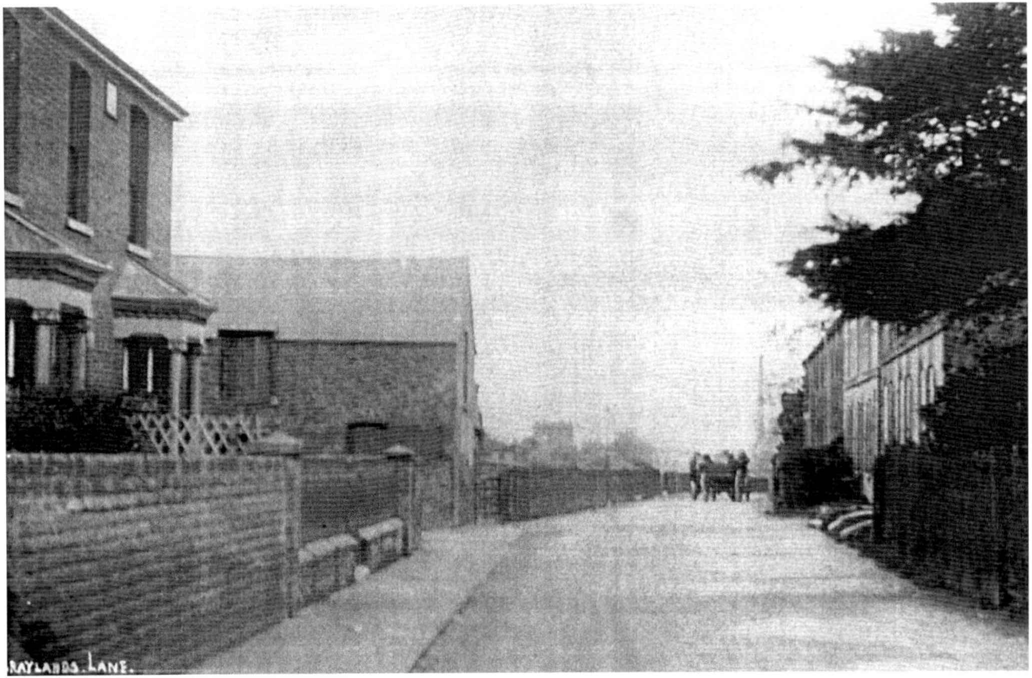

63. Craylands Lane, Swanscombe circa 1902. A view looking north from the junction with Milton Street. The pub on the right side (at end of row of cottages) was the Rising Sun – the only survivor of three public houses along this road (see picture 64). On the left is a Victorian detached house, which stood on the site of a former farm yard, which had barns and a hop kiln in the 1860s. During the 1930s it was used by Stone Court Ballast Company, but it is now demolished. The barn further along is the last survival of the farmyard of Crown Farm and behind the barn was one of the many allotments in Swanscombe. The present-day Swanscombe Centre (which includes the Swanscombe & Greenhithe Town Council offices) was opened in 1989 on a site to the left of the cart shown in the picture.

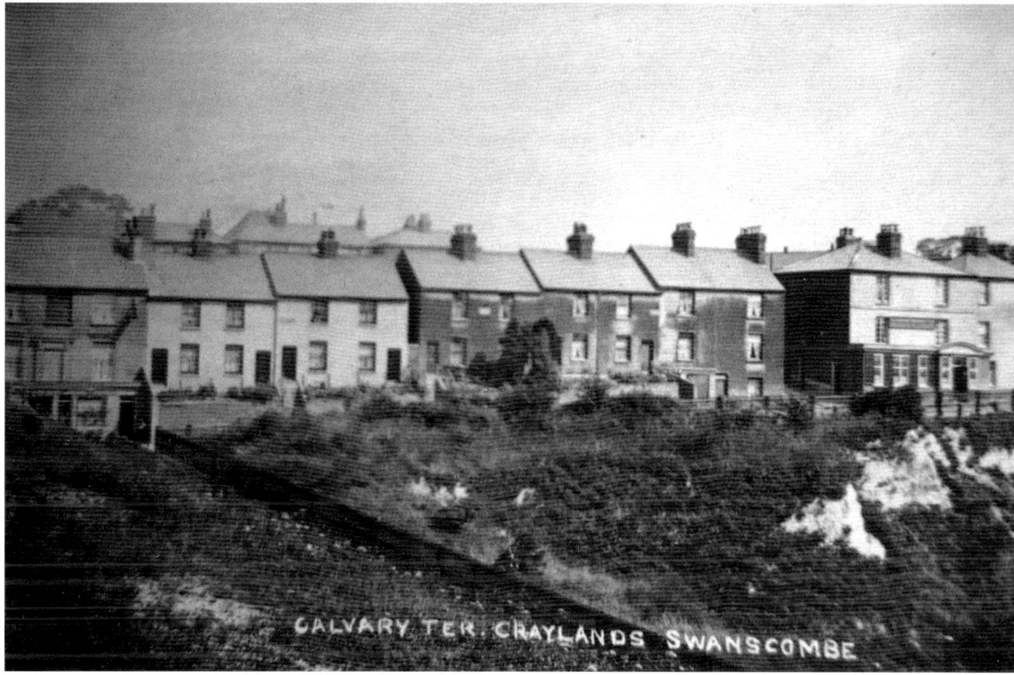

64. Calvary Terrace, Craylands Lane, Swanscombe circa 1905. Craylands Lane is an ancient road linking the hamlet of Milton Street with the main Gravesend to Dartford road (A226) at Swanscombe Cross, directly opposite to the main entrance to the Cement Works. This area was developed by the needs of the cement workers and the houses dated from the 1850s and 1860s. It was developed into a little community with 3 public houses – two are shown here. On the extreme left is the Coopers Arms (known locally as the 'Bottom House'). The large building on the right of the picture (next to the alleyway) was the North Kent (known as the 'Middle House') and beyond that, towards Milton Street, was the Rising Sun (the 'Top House') – outside of this view. All 3 pubs were in operation until after the Second World War – only the Rising Sun remains. The alleyway, seen next to the North Kent led to Craylands Square, another Victorian creation consisting of some 15 or so small cottages and houses. This whole area was redeveloped in the very early 1970s and replaced by housing of that period.

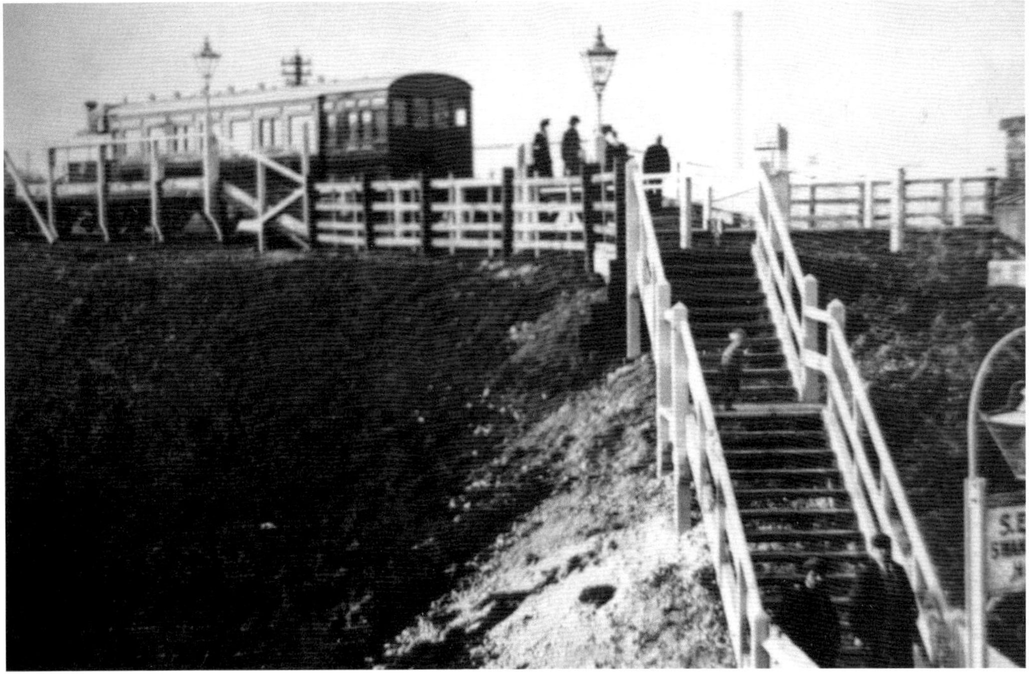

65. Swanscombe Railway Halt, Craylands Lane. This was the first railway station exclusively for Swanscombe and it was opened in 1908. The service was provided for the ever-increasing population but it was constructed in an inconvenient position for most residents in an isolated location away from the most populous area. The South East & Chatham Railway provided this as an extra service once they had managed to halt plans to amalgamate the Gravesend and Dartford tramways and so maintaining their control on travel to London. Swanscombe Halt's Craylands Lane site was closed and moved to its present position in the High Street in 1930 – but the entrance steps (now bricked up) can still be seen today. The original halt was one without toilets, which was another problem with it. The train shown is a rail motor where the steam engine is part of the whole vehicle. These ran between Gravesend & Dartford but were not successful as they could not cope with extra carriages and if the locomotive broke down the whole train was useless and inflexible.

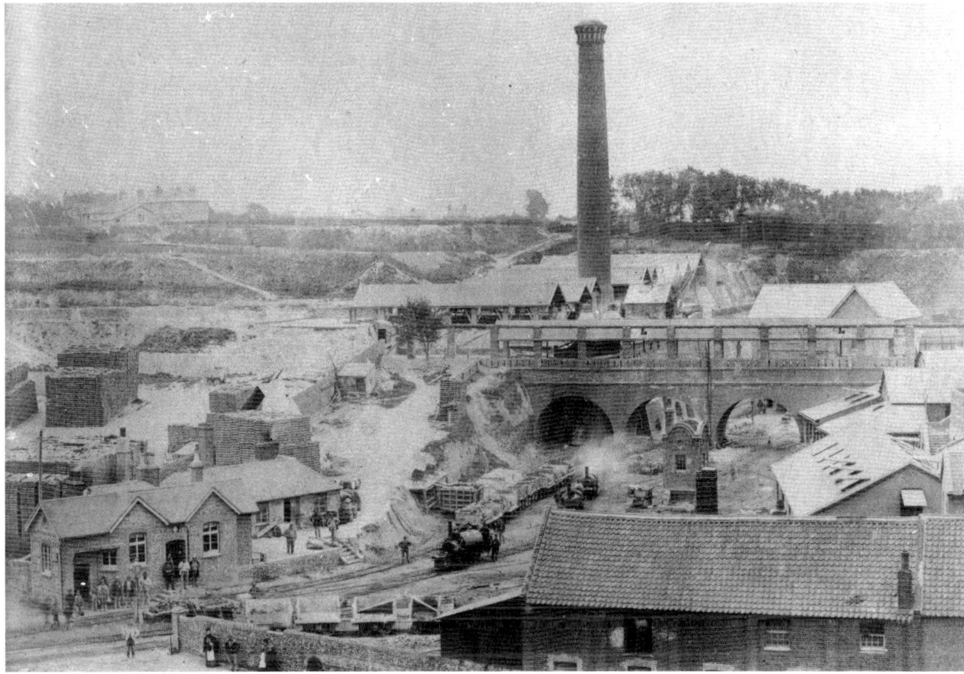

66. Swanscombe Cement Works circa 1872. This is the earliest photograph of the Cement Works in this book. The view is looking south across the works towards Galley Hill. This was the primitive Cement Works that had developed since the 1820s and consequently the pollution from it was appalling leading to a campaign in 1874 to close the factory. A monster rally was organised to counter this proposal to which some 5,000 men, women and children were drawn. One cement worker spoke of the wealthy men who wanted to stop the pollution as 'cursed with too much time. If those rich neighbours... had closer acquaintance with the privations of the poor and could see their sometimes starving families, they would not feel the smoke a nuisance'. The cement workers were led by Reverend Thomas Candy, the rector of Swanscombe, and a brass band with the men at the front of the rally carrying sticks with loaves of bread impaled upon them – to symbolise the Cement Works providing food for workers. Mr. S.C. Umfreville of Ingress Abbey and other wealthy landowners were the promoters of the cement factory closure – it was cement that won that argument and its consequent influence is everywhere in Swanscombe.

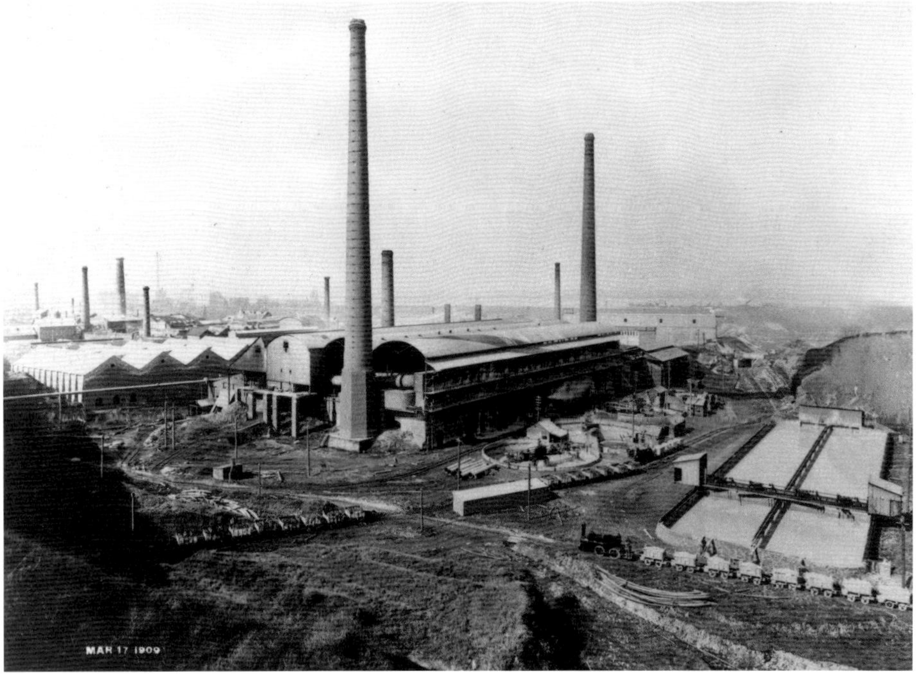

67. Swanscombe Cement Works, 1909. The single most important institution in changing the physical and social face of Swanscombe was unquestionably the Cement Works, opened on the edge of the marshes in 1825. The Cement Works became wholly owned by the White family in 1838 and grew from a small and primitive establishment into a vast industrial area creating urban Swanscombe and huge swathes of pits and despoiled land in its wake. The Cement Works were constantly developing and updating – this picture is quite different to the one of 1872 and to latter ones in the never ending search for efficiency and profits. In 1900-1901 the new revolutionary rotary kilns replaced the existing technology and even the great flood of 1953 only stopped production for five days before all kilns were fully functioning. In 1970 when all the local cement works were closed and production unified at the new Northfleet Works, Swanscombe alone survived manufacturing special cement products such as 'Snowcrete'. The decline in demand for cement in 1989-1990 caused by the government's economic slump coupled with the ever worsening ability to dig for chalk and clay locally, caused Swanscombe Works to close in 1990, and its consequent demolition.

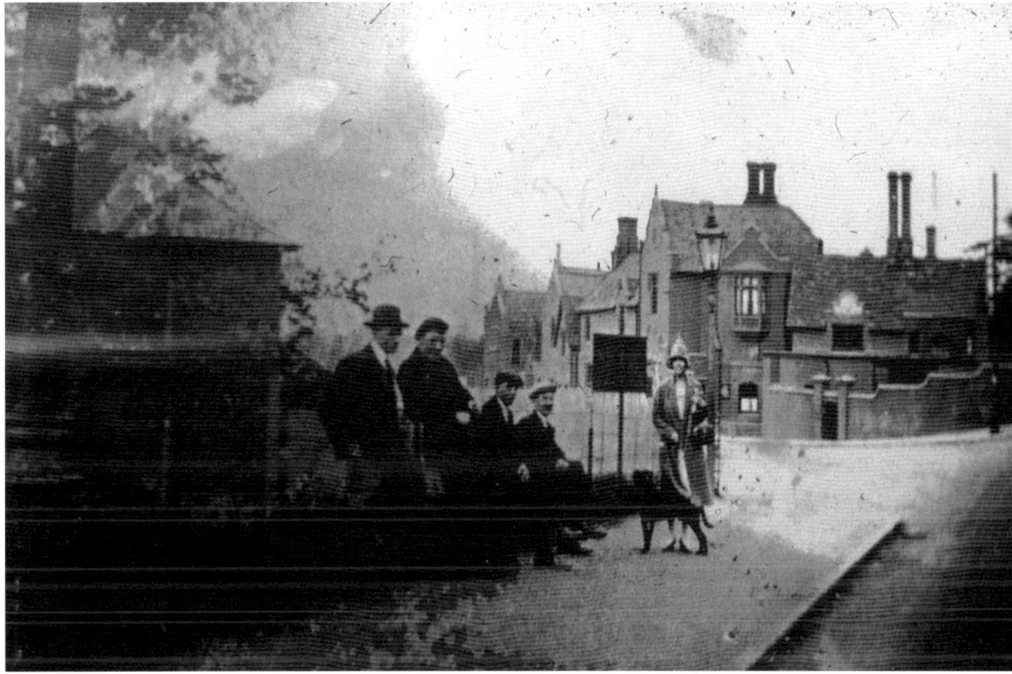

68. Entrance to Swanscombe Cement Works circa 1924. The view shows the house built by John Bazley White, whose family first became partners in Swanscombe Cement Works in 1833. In about 1838 Bazley White built a house for himself at the entrance to his source of fortune, and in Victorian style he was heavily involved in community projects within Swanscombe. Examples of these projects were the establishing of Galley Hill School, All Saint's Church, Galley Hill and Swanscombe Literary Institute. White's grip on Swanscombe was very firm – he controlled matters with his power as a major employer, a major landowner and used his wealth to support community groups he felt would help his control in Swanscombe. As a Victorian 'Lord of the manor', White would bully the Parish Council or others over rate payments or similar matters. The area shown here was known as 'Swanscombe Cross' – the cross being the meeting of London Road, Craylands Lane and the Cement Works entrance. From 1902 until 1929 this area was the terminus of the Gravesend Tramways system, which brought workers to the gates of the Cement Works, before returning up Galley Hill back to Northfleet and Gravesend.

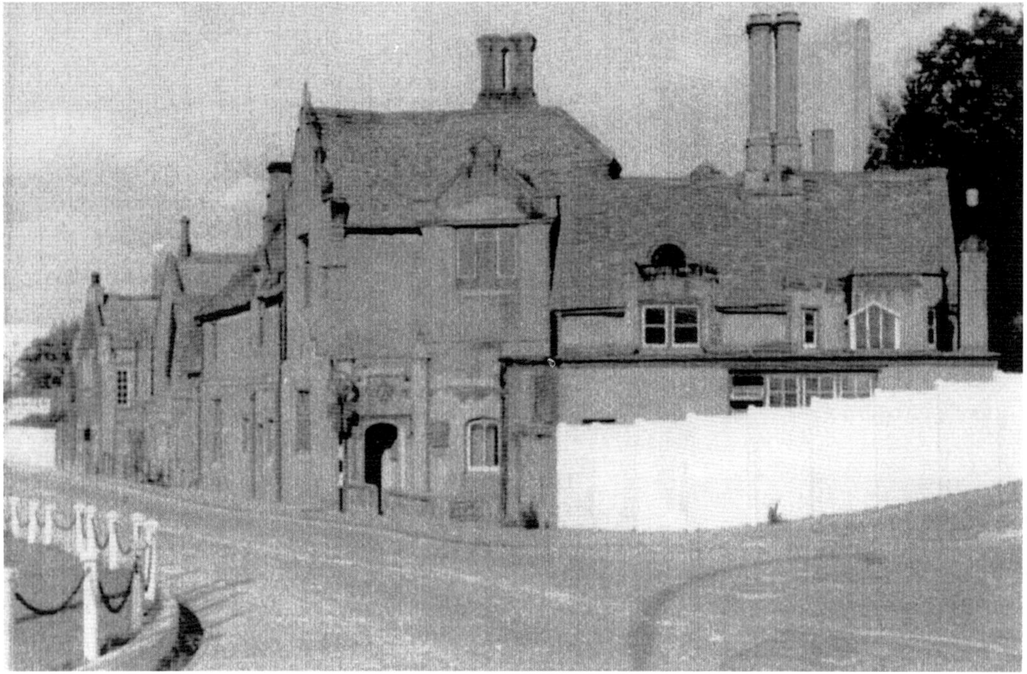

69. John Bazley White's House, Swanscombe Cross. Undoubtedly the most important private dwelling in Swanscombe associated with the cement industry. The house stood at the entrance to the Cement Works – the right of this building was London Road leading to Galley Hill, while the left led straight into the works. John Bazley White had this strange mixture of architectural styles built in the early Victorian years and it was believed to be one of the earliest buildings made from concrete. The Whites moved out and the exterior modified later in the nineteenth century. In September 1926 the building was leased by the Associated Portland Cement Manufacturers (the organisation founded in 1900 uniting many independent cement factories) to the newly created Swanscombe Urban District Council – it was known as 'No. 1 Factory House' – neither imagination nor historical accuracy were ever great traits of the cement industry! Swanscombe Council was paying APCM a rent of £100 per annum plus £13 for an additional room in 1944. Swanscombe Urban District Council vacated the house in 1964 and subsequently this important building was demolished and replaced with waste ground.

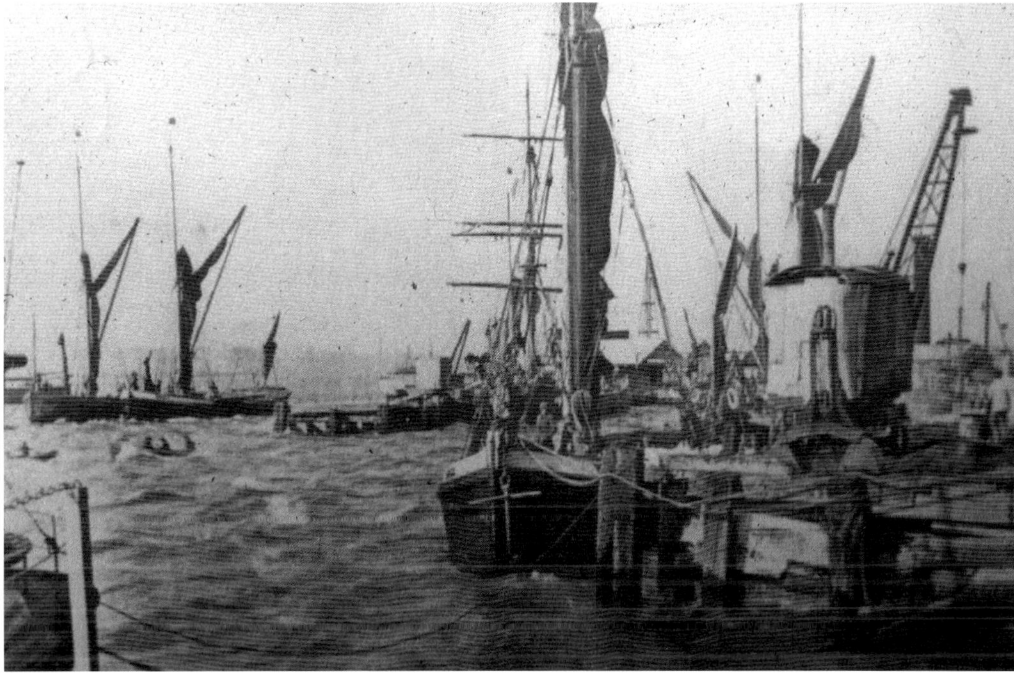

70. Swanscombe Cement Works – White's Wharf circa 1910. This busy view shows the River Thames when it was an extremely well-used international waterway before the decline of the 1960s onwards. White's Wharf (named after the owners of the Cement Works but formerly known as Bull's or Bell's Wharf) was used to import clay and export finished cement along the railway, which connected the river and the Cement Works. The picture illustrates Thames barges and a steam crane in operation – the cement would have been exported in barrels rather than the later cement sacks. In addition to cement, whiting (a fine powder made from specially selected chalk) was also exported from Swanscombe for use in paint, linoleum, chemical and rubber industries. Before 1939 whiting was exported to France for tooth and face powder. Flints (a waste product of chalk excavation) were also exported for use in pottery or in a crushed state for use in chemical products.

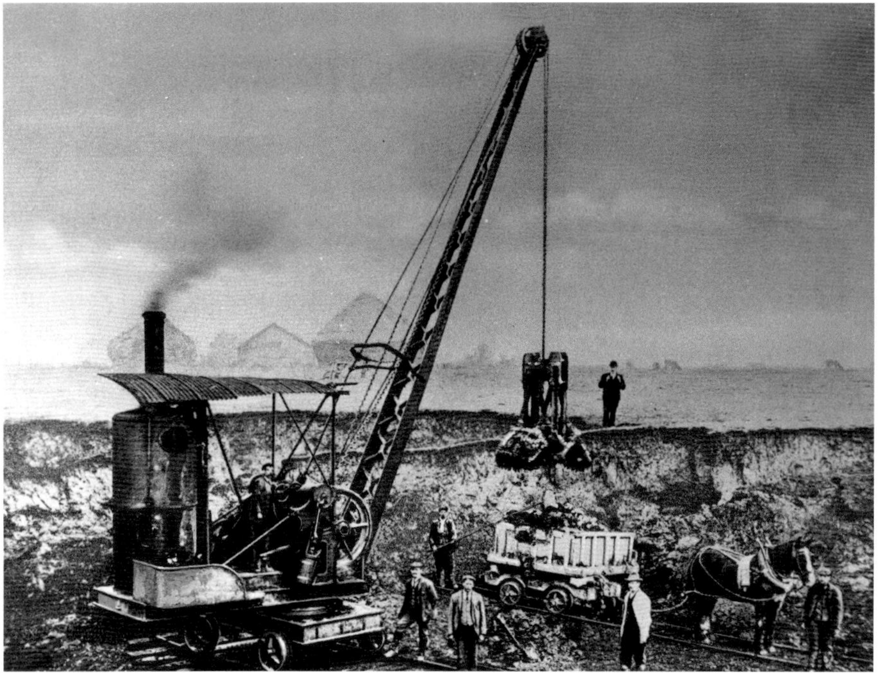

71. Steam grabber removing soil circa 1903. An example of 'new' technology: the use of steam machinery for the removal of agricultural land at Swanscombe. This view shows the field in rear including a barn and hay stacks and illustrates clearly how Swanscombe was ever changing from agriculture to industry at this time. In 1872 the manor of Swanscombe was purchased by Thomas Bevan, a cement manufacturer of Northfleet, and consequently in 1900 became the property of the APCM (Associated Portland Cement Manufacturers). The land was rented to farmers until it was needed for cement manufacture when the topsoil was removed in order to win the chalk or clay below. This photograph is believed to be in the area around Baker's Hole running along the Ebbsfleet Valley.

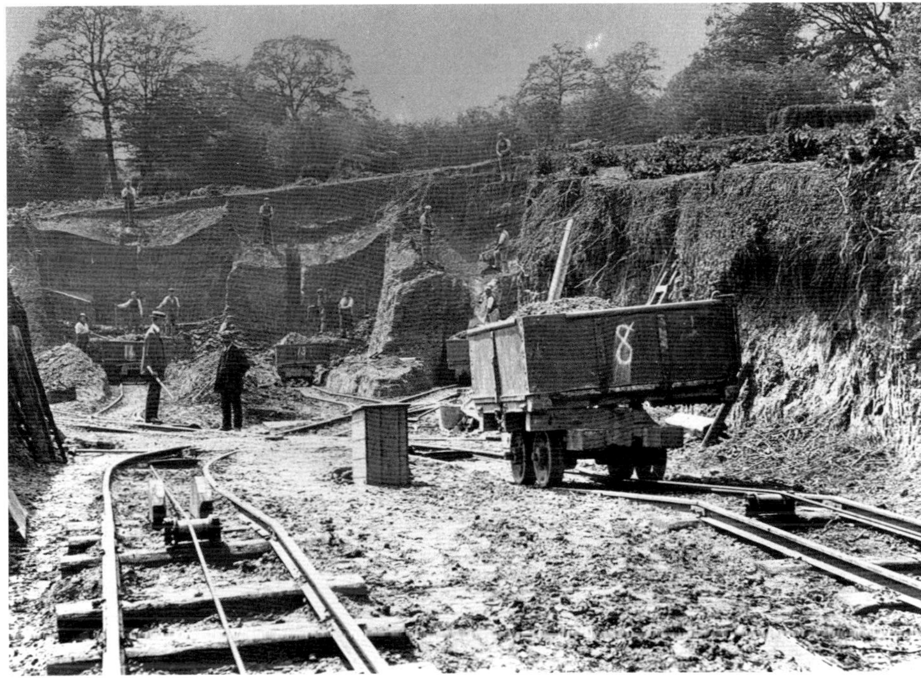

72. Excavation of sand, gravel and clay, Swanscombe Woods circa 1925. This excavation is believed to be in Swanscombe Woods and is part of the cement industry's need for clay, chalk and other minerals. It was excavations such as these, which destroyed one of Swanscombe's great historical features known as 'Sweyne's Camp' in 1928. This feature was a man-made mound created as a motte for a Norman stockade type castle guarding the nearby Watling Street. Likewise, Swanscombe Woods as a whole were destroyed by excavation for clay and chalk. Pits such as these revealed a wealth of prehistoric remains and man-made implements, which brought Swanscombe to the attention of many archaeologists. One of the most famous was Henry Stopes, father of Marie Stopes, the pioneer of family planning in the 1920s.

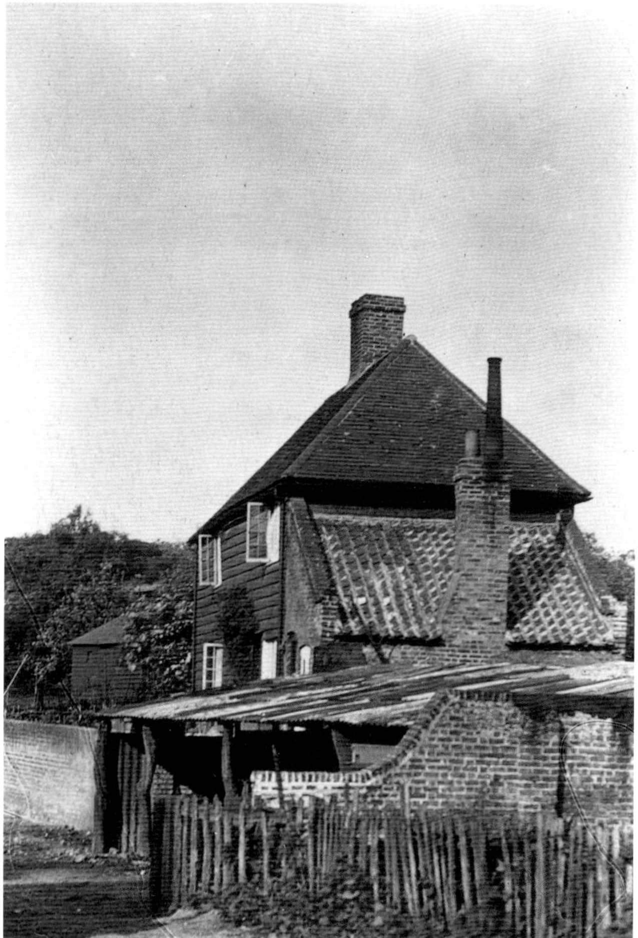

73. Alkerden Farm, Swanscombe. Alkerden (pronounced locally as 'Arkeden') is the name of an ancient manor in Swanscombe and the farm nestles in a small valley on the south-western outskirts of the town. The view shown is dated around 1895 and shows the farmhouse that existed in the seventeenth and eighteenth centuries and served as the farmers' house until the 1950s when the present house was built in an adjacent position. The old farmhouse shown here declined into being a barn and storage area. The farm was engaged in fruit growing during the late nineteenth and early twentieth centuries to feed the ever increasing demand for market gardening from the London market. In 1872 the house was sold to Thomas Bevan, the cement manufacturer, and since then the farm has been owned by the cement industry giant APCM, later Blue Circle – the farmer is a tenant of the company. The manor was also known as 'Coombs' and was already mentioned in documents during the 1320s.

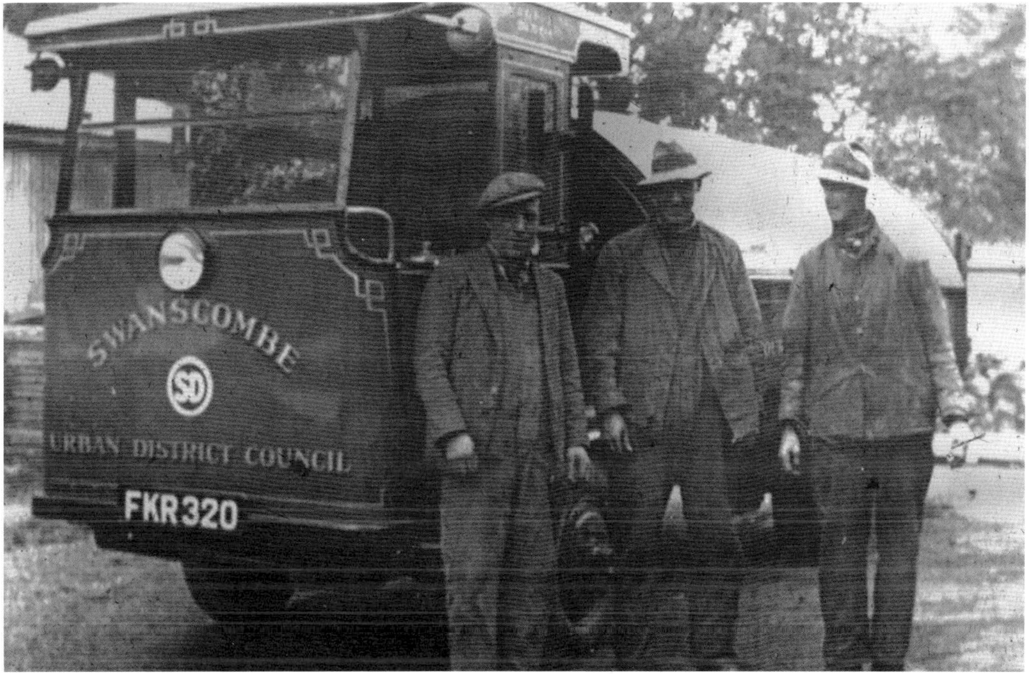

74. Swanscombe Urban District Council Dust Cart, circa 1939. A great symbol of municipal pride was the dust-cart emblazoned in the council's livery. The above was registered in 1939 and was a dustless loader, petrol-driven freighter manufactured by Shelvoke & Drury. Rubbish was collected from the rear of properties via the network of alleyways and then loaded into the carts, which had a terrific choice of pits in which to dump Swanscombe and Greenhithe's refuse. The main pit was a disused chalk quarry at the rear of Barnfield Pit, off Craylands lane. Swanscombe Urban District Council's refuse service is remembered for its efficiency and the council had already been using motor vehicles since 1930 when an Eagle-Thornycroft refuse cart was purchased to modernise the horse drawn fleet.

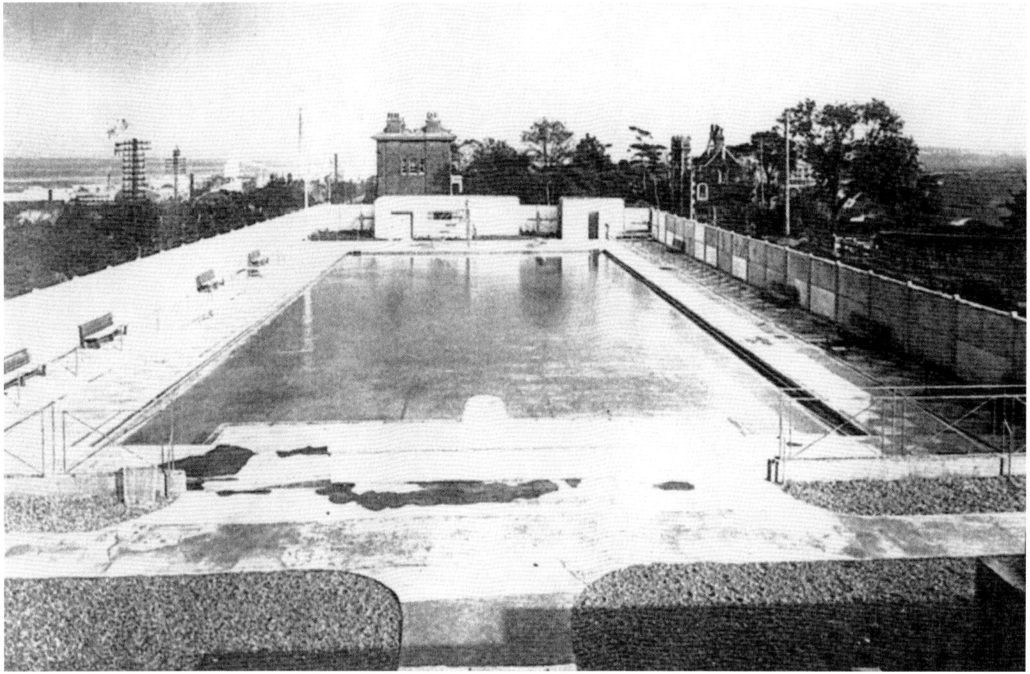

75. Swanscombe swimming pool, London Road. Swanscombe Urban District Council was dedicated to its task of improving life for ordinary people in what was a heavily industrialised area. The council's motto, often referred to in this book, was making 'a better and brighter Swanscombe' during the 1920s and 1930s – and part of this movement included the open-air swimming pool opened on 8th August 1936 at a cost of £5,800. Swanscombe's swimming pool was ahead of Dartford, Gravesend and Northfleet in its modernity and it was a source of universal community pride that a small town was able to provide such a marvellous facility. In succeeding years, however, the neighbouring towns were able to provide modern indoor pools during the 1970s and it was with great sadness and even greater anger that Dartford Borough Council, who had become the council responsible for much of the urban district's great achievements in 1974, closed the pool in 1982 and sold the site for housing. The provision of a new leisure centre in Swanscombe in 1989 still failed to silence the murmurs of Swanscombe's deeply hurt civic pride.